BACK AND FORTH

POEMS BY TONY HENDRY

First Edition: *Back and Forth / Poems by Tony Hendry*

ISBN: 978 1 7396674 2 9

First published in the UK in 2023 by Caldew Press.

Caldew Press
Tolivar
12 St George's Crescent
Carlisle
CA3 9NL

www.caldewpress.com

Printed and bound in Great Britain by Clays Ltd, Elcograf S.p.A.

CALDEW PRESS

FOREWORD

It is over a year now since we lost our brother Tony. The family, for whom he was 'the rock', miss him greatly, as I'm sure many of his friends do. As you may have heard me say before, Tony – at the tender age of just 68 – was really getting into his stride in many ways and some terrific years were ahead of him. Sadly, it was not to be.

Happily, Tony will leave us with some great memories and his talent as a poet will stay with us forever. He was so proud when his first collection of poetry (*Fresh Air*) was published and now we have *Back and Forth*, a collection of his more recent work, that we can all enjoy. I'm sure he (as his family are) would be equally proud of it. In this collection, we get to see more of Tony the person and the challenges he faced as well his unique and quirky view of everything around him.

How did *Back and Forth* come about? Well, one of his last instructions to me, in very wobbly handwriting, was to make sure his post *Fresh Air* portfolio of work reached his friend Phil Hewitson. Phil and the family were of the same mind, that if a posthumous publication of his work was possible, we would do it. When I say we…

Inevitably, bringing a collection like Tony's to life involves some serious hard work – and time – and the family owes a huge debt of gratitude to two people. Phil Hewitson, whom most of you will know, has patiently collated and edited Tony's work to create *Back and Forth* as we see it now while our cousin Hunt Emerson has once again produced some brilliant artwork that manages to enhance Tony's wonderful words.

So, a huge thanks from the family to Phil and Hunt and of course the Caldew Press, without whom *Back and Forth* would not have happened.

Finally, if I may, I would like to dedicate this collection to all of Tony's friends and colleagues from the SpeakEasy and other poetry groups that supported him and brought him confidence and joy in his latter years.

Also, because he is not here, let's dedicate *Back and Forth* to the man himself, Tony Hendry.

Rob and Chris Hendry

EDITOR'S NOTE

On Friday 21st January 2022, in what was almost his final message to me, Tony wrote, 'Bit of a rum do with my pan-creatic cancer. When dust has settled you may want to look through my Back and Forth collection… will get it to you via brother Chris.'

Now, here it is – *Back and Forth* – along with a selection of other poems by a most talented writer, poet and much missed friend to all who knew him, particularly in the Carlisle and Cumbria poetry and folk music scenes.

Special thanks to Chris, Rob and all the Hendry family. Huge thanks also to Hunt Emerson, who has returned to illustrate *Back and Forth* after providing such wonderful drawings for Tony's previous collection *Fresh Air*.

Thanks also to Janette Fisher, Jane Lucy, Becca Roberts, Barbara Renel, John Luffrum and Malcolm Carson for sharing Tony's poems and helping make this collection happen.

Phil Hewitson

CONTENTS

Back

Forth

Poems by Tony Hendry

BACK

Catstycam And Helvellyn

Steep steps, but the handrail helped.
Catstycam, Helvellyn from the attic,
past the estate and Carlisle racecourse.
Her policeman son has told her off –
don't, mum, you'll have a fall one day.
But, bless him, he was never young,
just as his dad, her man, was never old,
no matter what the liver spots might say.

Near the end, recalling mountain days,
sub zero larks, bumslides on hard snow,
crashing into drifts, then her pelting him
with snowballs. Rough wooing, she said.
Should have dumped you there and then,
he said, with that smile she missed most.
Wedding stipulation: white confetti only.
Off on honeymoon through a blizzard.

Catstycam and Helvellyn in view.
Touch the window pane, resolve.
Sensible son would be expecting her
to study the brochures he had left.
Sheltered housing, central, near shops
and surgery, no views to hurt or soothe.
But the last job her man did for her
was to put that handrail up.

Adult Social Care

Colder winters. Old bones ache.
Black ice pavements terrorise.
Last week I tried those grippers,
but still I went arse over tip.
Shut indoors for fear of slipping,
I wait for neighbours to offer lifts.
I used to rove the snowy fells,
but I won't go there no more.

Springs are windier. Eyes stream.
I tell neighbours I'm not crying
when I cross them in the street.
If I were a bud I'd stay unfurled.
This was once the best of times.
I'd bivouac in the greening wood
and watch badger cubs at dawn,
but I won't go there no more.

These days, summer brings yobs.
Hot nights, joyrides, lobbed cans.
I hear the gangs use baseball bats.
Neighbours tell me not to worry,
but the old chap found in the river
had a stoved-in skull, or so I heard.
I used to fish that river after work,
but I won't go there no more.

Autumns are wetter and wilder.
The pelting rain stings and soaks.
Once, I'd have raised my face to it.
Neighbours contacted the council.
A girl's brolly drips in the porch
as she talks of assessing my needs.
Black tights, a ladder on a thigh.
I'd have flirted with her, once,
but I won't go there no more,
no I won't go there no more.

Missing

What's that word?
What's that choice word,
when rain falls on dry soil
and earthy scent fills the air?
Petrichor. Well done, sir.
Brain, sense of smell intact.
Vision, too: tufts of grass,
base of a hedge, rusty can.
Mobility's another matter.
Head, limbs, torso all still.
Can't even flex my fingers.

I suppose I asked for it.
Night rambling, country lane,
trusting in narrow verges,
just like in the old days.
A van hit me. Not a wallop,
a glancing blow to the hip.
Don't know if the driver knew,
but the van sped on like crazy.
I was so shocked and dizzy,
that I crumpled there and then
as the soft rain came on.

The rain's gone, and I'm here,
free to wallow in petrichor.
Same as before, now and then,
at bivouacs at dawn or dusk
on intrepid treks in wild land.
Plant oil plus soil bacteria,
or fluid from the veins of gods,
it's making me feel… as one.
No cars yet on this quiet lane.
At this rate, I'll be a bulletin –
man missing from care home.

Fashion Lapses

I will wear a brown cardigan
with buttons of imitation horn
and two sagging side pockets
for butterscotch and bogies.

I will wear elasticated trousers
with room for a swelling belly.
Their colour will be charcoal,
to hide expected slitter stains.

I will wear fawn slippers
with lining of imitation wool.
A size too big, so they flap
as I learn my old man shuffle.

I will put on these purchases
and be enraged. I will photo
my inverse in the hall mirror
to capture this awful instance

of clothes unmaking a man,
then run upstairs to strip off
and get back into gangrel kit
abandoned during the bother.

I will stuff my fashion lapses
in my rucksack, march them
at the double up a mountain,
and burn them by the cairn.

I will warm hands at the fire as
sparks fly towards Crummock,
then my ageing bones will creak
as I leave the pyre to smoulder.

I will manage the long descent.

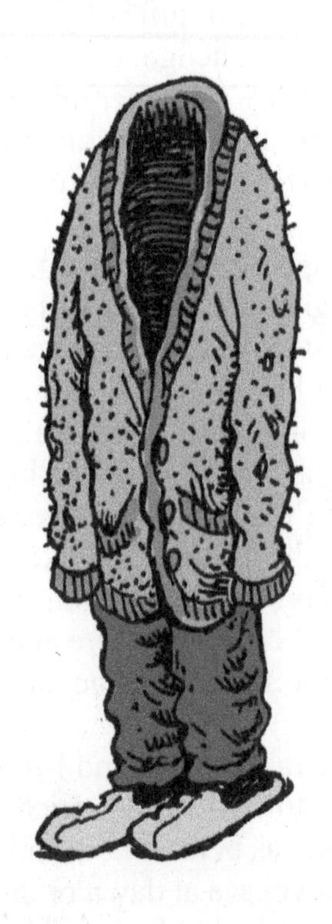

Outpaced

Not like you expected.
No single set of footsteps,
rhythmic, never pausing,
steadily catching up.

Four feet are behind you.
Now and then, they stop
as if to tantalise you...
yet still they catch you up.

Don't. Look. Back.
Do not quicken your pace.
Risking a blow to the skull
is better than losing face,

old chap.
Then a young couple pass,
lad and lass, sharing songs,
linked by white earphones,

hands in the back pockets
of each other's blue jeans,
cheerfully squeezing bums.
You are invisible to them.

This is a long old street,
and they will keep stopping
for kisses, and the first time
you're near enough to hear

the smack of parting lips.
They're not being nasty,
it's just that you're invisible.
Time, in their persons, has

casually passed you by.
As the gap grows and grows,
you can only keep going
your way, at a steady pace.

St Ninian's Well

Brisco was Birksceugh,
clearing in a birch wood.
Now, past neat cottages,
empty winter fields fall
to a fast-flowing river.
I come upon a holy well
named for a Pictish saint.
A beguiler, lost in myth
since the Romans left.

The wellhead excites.
A romanesque arch
in worn local sandstone
over rough square trough.
But my know-all phone
lacks all imagination –
early Victorian, it says.
Yet there's a holly tree
giving evergreen hope.

So here stands Ninian,
starting a mission north
by a stream in a clearing.
He is curer, purifier,
blesser and baptiser
on this Candlemas day,
when water from his cup
is cold enough to make
babes and old folk gasp.

Patiently, I wait in line.
But when the phone rings
I must step aside, and now
I'm talking with a nurse,
settling a time and date
to talk through test results.
Fate unknown, saint gone,
yet I am not abandoned.
I walk on to the river.

Always Alive

He found it behind other plants
on a sun-starved lower shelf
in a rundown garden centre.
No how to grow on the label,
just the name, *sempervivum,*
which he liked.

He paid for it by contactless,
and saw his hand was shaking.
Always alive sounded good.
An autumn of brown envelopes
falling through his letterbox,
bearing Infirmary summonses.

He planted his newfound ally
near the middle of a raised bed
with plenty of room to grow.
Rough start. Within a week,
its two offsets broke and died.
Now, just one green rosette

of maybe thirty tufted leaves,
and he'll fret for all of them.
But online study gives hope.
A frost-resistant succulent
which keeps leaves in winter.
A rapid spreader.

Culpeper, the herbalist,
said a posset of its juice is
singularly good in hot agues.
Handy, if the meds go wrong.
Of other names, the best is
Jupiter's Beard.

Grown on roofs, they say,
to ward off bolts of lightning
from that quick-to-anger god.
Flowers don't come for years,
but, in the circumstances,
he can always live with that.

In Twenty Years

In laureled avenues by the park,
in streets named after aldermen,
along the flower-potted walkways
of tower blocks, and all over town

the carers call in ones and twos.
Between turning off their vapes
and turning on their cheery faces,
the ones press bells and buzzers

or rap out riffs with letterbox flaps.
The twos, paired to manoeuvre,
talk of unfair rotas then turn keys
or tap in numbers on access pads.

Seen-it-alls in sensible tunics,
punctuators of the screed of days
for those kept out of sight and mind,
these couthy, undervalued women

scare me. Their medical gloves
may rest upon me soon enough.
However many clinics I attend,
the carers may come calling soon.

Low hills loft beyond the town,
then a mountain with a hidden corrie
where deer-cropped emerald grass
is a perfect pitch for my old tent,

and the carers would never find me.
Some nights I'm there in dreams,
then it's birdsong in the rosy dawn
and ambrosia porridge by the burn.

Back

Look, the plovers are back.
Our long-lost wintering friends,
on fellside past the intake wall,
plumage showing flecks of gold
in perfect morning sunlight.

The path by the sparkling beck
is a marvel, single track again,
as if the footfall of these decades
never happened. Our eyes widen.
Where is this day taking us?

Up on the ridge, the long view
over the Solway Plain looks odd.
I rack my brain, and work it out:
towns chuff smoke into the sky
and the wind turbines have gone.

Our clothes are wool once more,
and you are my lady in tweeds.
Near the top, you dig out the map,
though we know the way so well.
Metric's gone. Each square a mile.

I find I'm aching less than usual,
can walk and talk without panting,
tell you the stuff I can't tell others.
You'd rather we listen to the wind,
but let me blether, as kind as ever.

Now we are at the summit cairn.
I take your hand and raise it high
in triumph at being back with you,
back again on a joyful morning,
before you left so early.

Talking To Cecilia

Wuk, they call it in this town.
Glad to have a job where many don't,
they tilt their chins up as they say
Can't stop, Songman, I'm off to wuk,
or *Not Saturday, lad, I'm wukking.*
For better or worse, it's wedlock.

Overalls or supermarket smocks,
office suits or yellow high viz vests,
all uniforms are worn with quiet pride.
Wuk is canteen natter, doing it right,
banter with bosses, steadiness, skill,
not fretting when you buy a round.

They'd stomp the toad into the ground
some days. *Lad, I'm sick to death of wuk.*
Roll on retirement. But when wages stop
and pensions start, wuk is kept close.
Gardens, grandkids, repairs and classes
protect them from being sick or sad.

So it is with me. By the way, a lad
in Carlisle can be six or sixty odd.
Guess which I am, lass? I mine my head
and wuk on songs which may get sung
after my molecules have moved along.
If not? The lad did all he could.

Saint Cecilia, help me to be good.

Lump

In the last daylight hour of the winter solstice,
the task I choose, or the task chosen for me,
is to unblock the drain in my back yard.

In tramp clothes, wearing gardening gloves,
I kneel on flagstones, remove the drain cover,
and dip a plastic tumbler into brimming gunk.

Pint by disgusting pint, the level is dropping.
The stuff I transfer into two red buckets
is brown water, leaf mulch, and growing blobs

of fat (beads, marbles, golf balls) which glow
maggot white even under sullen skies.
Otherworldly rancid stench assaults me.

With the level low, I use a rusted iron hook
to gouge away from the hidden outflow grille
a turnip-sized lump of fat which makes me gag.

Once it is bucketed, and the bucketfuls
irresponsibly poured on waste ground,
I grin into the dusk at a job well done.

From tomorrow, water will flow unblocked
as days stretch towards another solstice.
My friend's tumour will respond to chemo,

and all will be made well.

I Feel Sick

So many ways to vomit,
and so much need to emit.
Each gobbet of horror news,
served by suit or flak jacket,
acts as an emetic.

Look, more old butchery.
More slaying and massacre
as peace talks folded.
Look, another mum cradling
a bloodsoaked bundle.

Was it always thus?
Was there always a point
when tender souls like ours
could thole it no longer,
and had to chunder?

We vomit through ages
at violence to innocents.
Heaving, hurling, barfing,
spewing, puking, boking.
Such blowing of chunks,

such unquenchable flow
through gullets and mouths
to all those affronted floors.
Recent meals looking like
our diced insides.

We are hollowed out,
with just enough strength
to slalom past sick pools
to reach our back garden
or nearest patch of green.

Breezes cool our sweat,
and our stomachs settle.
Saliva returns. We swill
and spit out remnants.
Now we look around.

Bird, bough, bud, bloom,
none sharing our nature.
They go about business
purely. We are ignored
and nourished.

Near Woldingham

Once, two fox cubs tumbled down a slope
in a playfight, to come to a halt at your feet.
All three of you were astounded.

Once, a white hart ambled out of folklore
to cross a field between two beech woods.
Never seen again in twenty years.

Always, the liberation of gaining height
until you hit the scarp and the broad view,
and anything was possible.

Except, of course, on all the shrouded days.
They were like the storm-felled tree trunks
that you had to clamber over.

No sure delights. Fat mud could clog boots
and burden you like thoughts about last week
and fears about the week to come.

No sure delights, so you cherished them more.
Leaf litter bronzed by winter sun, emerald moss,
blood clot holly berries in old marl pits.

You were always alone, yet sometimes sharing.
There was a bench inscribed for a young man
who loved to work with wood,

and often you said hello at the school graves,
where two forever teenaged girls lay down
with nuns of the Sacred Heart.

At times of loss, you gripped invisible hands
and asked their owners to look at the view.
Look across the Weald, you'd say,

to Ashdown Forest, and the South Downs.
Beautiful molecules shifting and settling.
We'll meet up by and by.

Big Mountain

All through the muggy morning,
we gain height but little distance.
The *sentiero's* white and red marks
on trunks of beech and holm oak
lead us on a punishment of zig zags,
each zag bringing us back above
the hill village of Costacciaro
where the bell of San Francesco
rings out the quarters.

Petulance worsens as we climb.
We kick beech mast at each other
and squabble over swigs of water.
When he claims the worst is over,
I say his lying got us here today.
He says I always slow him down.
Shut up. No, you shut up. Shut up.
Bright jays mock our childishness
as we carry on trundling.

At last, the zig zags lose tension
and relax into elegant curves.
Tree cover wavers, then gives up
at a grassy brow with wild horses
and a clear ridge to Monte Grande.
We eat bread, tomatoes and ricotta,
and tell the horses we'll get there.
Sisyphus and I are friends again,
and nothing without each other.

No Entry

A civil servant's lunch break.
Marsham Street exit, Smith Square,
and into Victoria Tower Gardens.
Past Rodin's Burghers Of Calais
to find the Thames in ebb or flow.
Sleek cormorants on yellow buoys.
On past worn grass at Palace Green
with its waltz of reporters and MPs.
Follow Westminster College wall
to Wippell & Co on Tufton Street,
near the Abbey, beside Faith House.
Supplier of ecclesiastical vestments
and furnishings for two centuries.

Window displays changed suddenly.
Chasubles with embroidered orphreys
were magicked into rose silk mitres
and silver croziers with dark oak stems.
Backlit stained glass roundels became
suspended brass and copper thuribles.
Legerdemain turned snowy surplices
scarved with black calf-length tippets
into gold-crossed burse and veil sets
to cover up the altar's sacred vessels.
Anglican gents from every continent
entered to examine naps and lustres
and emerged with bags and boxes.

Linger, always. Never enter.
The door, like faith, was shut to him,
but to look from outside was comfort.
Like plane tree leaves, cast bronze,
tides, primeval birds, obdurate grass
and old brick, it slowed heartbeat
and made life go a little easier.
Sometimes, for no reason, he'd work

past the rush hour, past evensong.
Michael, his boss, who prided himself
on being last one out of the office,
would poke his head around the door.
Have you got no home to go to?

None Of This Matters

None of this matters.
The sickly liqueur chocolate on the pillow
doesn't matter, nor the daftness of a balcony
overlooking a depot, nor the pleated loo roll,
nor the thick, grey top-of-the-wardrobe dust
discovered by her trailing index finger.

She shows him, then laughs at his dismay,
and says it doesn't matter. He's learning.
The puce curtains and the minibar robbery
don't matter, nor the potted palm restaurant,
nor the waiter who looks down her dress,
then denies it when he asks him to desist.

Hush, say her hazel eyes. Hushabye, my lad.
The bed is fine, and that's what matters.
We find each other and we lose ourselves,
we share our secrets and we trust each other,
and that's what matters, And, afterwards,
on lilac notepaper with a florid letterhead,

he lists what does and doesn't matter.
He nearly lost that list. Now, decades on,
when his poor choice of hotels has become
legendary, raised by their grown-up kids
at every family gathering, he looks at it again.
The years fall away. He starts to write.

Cold Air

Until this two-week cold snap,
I didn't know that polar air and arctic air
were different. Then, last night in fact,
while you were out, a sadist weatherman
said the cold northwesterly from Greenland
that had dipped the country into polar air
was giving way to even colder arctic air
straight from the flipping North Pole.
So turn the central heating up, he said.
Wear thermal underwear, and remove it
only when retiring early to your bed
with your partner. Snuggle up together
under a high tog duvet, and find fun ways
of generating heat.

He didn't say that, you said.
I may have embellished it a bit, I said
but why don't we have an early night
like, you know, like the way we did?
That look you gave. That long, level stare.
It was ominously colder than any arctic air.

Back To You

My senses are confused.
I hear wild garlic, smell granite,
and taste colour powder bombs
at a Holi festival in Bangalore,
though I've never been to India.

I see a frolicsome breeze,
a fox's bark, a tawny owl's hoot
and the burp of a contented baby
in a Tien Shan mountain village,
though I've not set foot in China.

I touch starlight and soundwaves,
savour the scent of the Jet Stream,
and listen to a batch of bagels
freshly made at a Chicago bakery,
though I've never been Stateside.

I was a prosaic stay-at-home,
but, since we met the other night,
my senses have become nomadic.
They move in Silk Road caravans,
in diving bells and on sky rockets,

on horses escaped from carousels,
and in mass molecular migrations.
Your smile has gifted me the world,
and different ways of knowing it,
yet everything leads back to you.

Sunny

Until it happened, he dwelt in comfort
in the nickname given by his mam.
From the start, his delight at the world
brimmed over into streams of laughter,
and the sun tangoed on tumbling water.
Her ray of sunshine, her laughing boy,
her laugh-a-minute lad. You are funny,
darling Sunny.

Forward through the gates of irony
which swung open at finger touch,
but now are bolted against retreat.
Behind his back, or even to his face,
neighbours and co-workers call him
Ray of Sunshine, or Laughing Boy,
or Laugh-A-Minute.

They reckon that he who was Sunny
is funny in the head. Now and then,
on the days he can't get out of bed,
he thinks of when Mam said he wore
rose-coloured spectacles. What's them?
he asked, but she didn't want to talk.
He never understood until it happened.

Low Pressure

Wish my friend a proper storm.
No quick kettledrum deluge
but the long whip of a warm front.
Number its lashes: four inches of rain,
seventy mile an hour rip of wind,
nine fifty millibars of pressure.

Wish him a good pitch
just halfway up the mountain.
A bank with just enough shelter
to stop his one-man tent
from kiting east to the coast
and across the surging sea.

Wish him a battling night,
hands pushing down tent pegs
or grasping the pole to stop a snap,
ears filled with mad flap of fabric,
eyes checking the seamsters' skill
which keeps the rain outside.

Wish him a restless, restful night,
a contented shaking in the womb
of a sporty third trimester mam
who knows her billowed body
and will release him easy
when he's due.

Wish him a proper storm
on his necessary mountain.
Let it scatter mobbing thoughts,
flush away the muck of fear,
and lull awhile the storm within.
Wish my young friend well.

Parental Guidance

A Cairngorms gully, fat with snow.
The right amount of give at first,
boots sinking in a couple of inches.
Grand, I thought, a fast way down
to a hot drink by the bothy stove.
Knowing my lack of common sense,
he followed quietly in my footsteps.
I'd be needing him soon enough.

Ankle-high, calf-high, knee-high,
and the gulley's flanks too steep now
to crab sideways onto safe slopes.
Then he began to talk. Right foot here,
left there, use the rock for balance.
Thigh-high now, but it's just a patch.
Try flopping like a sea lion for this bit:
use your hands and feet as flippers.

Easy, wasn't it? Ludicrous, but easy.
Piece of cake, like those we scoffed
back then, in the hills near the town.
Rest ten seconds, plough on for thirty.
Repeat, repeat, repeat. Keep sweating,
don't give in to the thought of sleep,
and, by the time you reach that rowan,
the snow will be back to ankle deep.

When I looked back, he wasn't there,
and his voice stilled, so soon I learned
to face the front as he talked me down.
My calm, sure bondsman of safety.
Beyond the rowan and out of danger,
his voice stopped dead. As before,
when slow to reach his hospital bed,
I was too late to say goodbye.

Leaving Early

You left the pubs and parties early,
before last round or last dance.
As crowds roared for encores at gigs,
you slid out to cool air and the way home.
When friends asked why, you found reasons –
the train won't wait, too many pints already.

You escaped, leaving the mess to others.
Samaritan types could bear the brunt.
Alleyway screams were not for your ears,
blood-splashed pavements not for your eyes.
Let other noses smell the sick and fear.
Can't slice my skin or break my bones.

Safe in the bedsit, you blocked the doubts.
The frozen lake you walked on, the dizzy ridge,
the forest bivouac when bears came foraging,
the famished fourteen-hour trek to road head,
the snow hole night, the mad Ulysses quests.
Such things were not for gutless cowards.

Yet the friends you left faced down
the small hours streets in mutual support.
Linked arms, took taxis, bared their souls,
offered beds and sometimes shared them.
Thus ménages and marriages bloomed,
then kids, then grandkids, and all.

Now you see your deeper cowardice,
to work so hard to miss all that
by leaving early.

Max

After university,
on a Master's in floundering,
I met Max through an agency
which found us work in dairies,
factories, fields and orchards.
Bussed-in yoghurt churners,
tattie pickers, crate stackers,
pittance earners.

It was all he could get after
six months for dealing drugs.
He tried for clean and straight,
saying he'd win the freedom
of the gallus house sparrows
we fed with crumbs in breaks.
He bit nails, sweated cobs,
got the shakes.

Dope didn't count for him.
He claimed it was medicinal.
Asked round, I saw a joint pass
from Max to the dead-eyed,
rake-thin dealing pals I found
he'd moved back in with. Said
No thanks, and never told him
what was yelling in my head –

Live in hostel, bothy, caravan,
sleep on my bedsit's filthy floor,
claim sanctuary at the church,
but get out of there, my friend!
It's never too late to change.
Soon I moved to another town,
as two waving arms were enough.
Things got better. I didn't drown.

I still feel bad I let Max down.

Stratford Season

In summer, in a Stratford season,
Alan Howard played Prince Hal,
and I was a porter and pot scourer
in the kitchen that made the meals
for punters who came to see him.

There was a hierarchy, of course.
Chef, sous chefs, on down to me,
just a lost youth of no account.
Nick and Eva were commis chefs,
an on-off item for a year or so.

Theatre of war, poisoned arrows.
That hot day, Nick was winning.
Like a baron retaking a castle,
he pushed Eva against a worktop,
grabbed her throat, simulated sex.

Chef grinned. Nobody spoke out.
Settle down. Yes chef, yes chef.
Eva's cheeks were glowing red
as she prepped the veg for lunch.
That was the way it was, then.

Once, I passed Bardolph, Poins
and Falstaff in a dim corridor.
Bardolph's nose was red as hell,
like a lamp for his companions,
or like a beacon to warn me.

But I couldn't escape my woes
or my youthful navel-gazing
to reach a better understanding.
I was trapped in that season.
The Henrys were blokeish plays.

Eva, would I speak out now,
if then was now and I was young?
I hope so, though I can't be sure.
Better to lose a hundred such jobs
than to feel this nagging shame.

Hopping

There was a notice at the student union
for vacation work – hopping down in Kent.
I travelled nervously to my Furthest South,
a farm by a village near Paddock Wood,
and claimed a bunk bed in a wooden hut.
Such a thing could never happen now.

Separate huts for students and East Enders.
Ours was a tip, but, judging by swept steps
and washed windows, theirs were clean.
We weren't invited in. They weren't hostile,
but this was their annual home from home
and we were one-offs who wouldn't return.

Deft matriarchs and their offspring
picked the hops with some student lasses,
I was among the luggers and processors.
Machines were coming in, but fingers still
turned green and smelt acrid yet floral.
Such a thing could never happen now.

The two groups united once, I think,
when the harvest was in, and a fire was lit,
and the farmer provided a barrel of beer,
and songs from the music halls were sung
as glowing sparks swirled into the night.
It's a fogged photo in my memory now,

except for Maria, a Poplar princess,
who had long black hair and kind eyes,
and didn't throw up at the sight of me.
There was just one hot kiss behind a hut,
the sort that ends too soon but lasts forever.
Such a thing could never happen now.

The Teens

Our numbers swell in this city.
Friends and family blank us,
and our devices stop working.
At our schools and colleges,
we bump into automatic doors
painlessly, till it gets tedious.
Then our involuntary crossings
wash us up in a raftered loft
high in a derelict warehouse.
We can see the shining Firth
through broken windows.

A full loft. Exits locked.
On a canvas sail of a screen,
we bewildered suicides
watch the images race by.
Cut wrists, mums and dads,
lambs frolicking in fields,
improvised nooses, dawns,
body parts on railway lines.
None of this can move us.
Nothing can hurt or gladden,
and soon our netted souls

are as calm as the lyre music
that drifts from the speakers.
A music student says Orpheus
is playing, and will free us soon.
Most of us have newer heroes,
and call on Batgirl, Wolverine,
The Hulk, or Wonder Woman.
A lass with a silver crucifix
and sea green eyes tells me
solemnly that this is Limbo,
and there will be a harrowing.

Mellbreak

Crow-black country nights.
Headlights sweeping narrow roads.
Callow drivers cornering too fast.
Unbelted passengers swaying, sliding.
Arms out of windows, palms tom-tomming
on rust-flecked Ford Cortina doors.

Many years ago this was,
before laminated Prove It cards,
when bar staff in Cumberland wilds
were more tolerant than those in town.
Friday nights, carloads of sixth formers
drove to the Kirkstile Inn and back

and, by a miracle, none died.
None were more alive than then,
when risk and beer slew devils.
Essays and swotting could wait.
Our respite, doing as we pleased,
like climbing Mellbreak at closing time.

Was it a bet or a dare? I forget.
Seven of us took up the challenge,
going *diretissima* by moonlight,
scaling the steep ridge behind the pub,
watched by scornful Herdwick sheep
and the silver eyes of two lakes –

Crummock Water, Loweswater.
Halfway up, I fell and gashed my wrist,
and the blood looked like black ink
by the moon. Two hankies staunched it –
mine tied to the one Lynn offered –
then onward to the summit cairn

which Luke reached first. Of course.
Hill farmer's son used to herding sheep,
county-standard runner, our top bloke.
High fives were yet to be invented,
so we all shook hands, jigged around
and howled in triumph at the moon.

My wrist still shows the scar.
Sometimes, on this sublunary path,
I track white bridge over blue vein
and recall swift, sure-footed Luke
back then on that Mellbreak climb.
First among us... to run out of time.

Type 2

Bright florin on the kitchen table.
Cupronickel, but good as silver
to a six-year-old that distant day.
A pocket money spat with Mam
made him think it was really his,
so he swiped it.

Hot as magma in trouser pocket.
In playtime breaks at infant school,
he took it out and doubts arose.
He asked the young queen's head,
but she was no help, so in the end,
on the way home,

he spent the lot at the sweet shop.
Candy cigarettes with red tips,
loads of them, munched in gobfuls
instead of being slowly "smoked".
Each pack had a swappable card
of a footballer.

Oh, those sherbert flying saucers!
Yellow, purple and lime green.
Softening rice paper with saliva,
then piercing the orb with tongue
for an always recollected explosion
of sweet shame.

Proof scoffed, he reached home,
but was never a match for Mam.
Inquisition, confession, tears,
bed after tea as initial sentence.
He and I, sweet tooth and guilt,
not getting away with it.

Egg Dumping In Cumberland

Mam boiled this pace egg
in a pan of red cabbage water,
and somehow it turned blue.
Magic, she said, that's how.

I call heads and lose the toss.
I hold the egg in my little fist,
only the blunt end showing.
I hope she boiled it enough.

I'm playing Snot Nose Ben.
Brown egg, onion skin dye.
He strikes with the sharp end,
too softly. Neither egg cracks.

Kids all over play this game
at Easter. *Tsougrisma* in Greece,
Eiertikken in the Netherlands,
Jarping on Tyneside, and so on,

but I don't know and don't care,
because I'm only six. My turn,
and I relax my wrist, and I focus
on the dead centre of the target,

and I strike from just three inches
with such deftness and precision
that the hit is like the firm click
of interlocking Lego bricks.

So how can *my* egg be cracked?
Why do *blue* flakes of shell fall?
Snot Nose is yelling in my face,
and all a little lad can do is race

home in tears. Drip, drip, drop.
Stop, says Mam. You're big now,
and big boys must learn to lose.
She makes an omelette for tea.

Chut

One of his nicknames was Chut.
Many years on, he wondered why,
and turned to his sisters for help.
Beth said grow up, idiot brother,
and Meg, his ever resilient Meg,
said never look back, you dimwit.

Undaunted, he mined lexicons,
and panned the streams of recall
for nuggets or flakes of gold.
Most results he quickly chucked.
For instance, he was sure he had
no precocious love of chutney;

had pointed from railway bridges
at choo choos, not chut chuts;
and had no way of knowing about
the Chut people living in Vietnam.
After all the mining and panning,
only two choices were left to him.

One was that chut chut chut chut
had voiced his deep contentment
as he nested in his mother's arms.
The other, supported by Chambers
in a sparse entry lacking sources,
was that chut had expressed

impatience. Maybe it was both.
Chick, then fledgling, then flight,
wasn't that just the way of things?
Too late to bring Mam back again,
to hug and let himself be hugged.
She'd have put him right, for sure.

Derwentwater's Farewell

JAMES RADCLYFFE, 3rd EARL OF DERWENTWATER

Slow air in the key of G.
The fiddle player summons
a floodtide of sweet sorrow
from horsehair and catgut.
The vinyl is nearing fifty.
The feet beating time
on a recording studio floor
in Hammersmith lead to
killing ground at Tower Hill.
Young James Radclyffe,
third Earl of Derwentwater,
is about to lose his head.
A Jacobite's last words.
He says he dies a Catholic
in charity with all the world.
He leaves a wife and baby.
Stepping north, far north,
to Derwentwater's home.
Dilston Hall, near Corbridge,
south of Hadrian's Wall.
And, in the blink of an eye
after the welling of a tear,
a new hall in the grounds
is a maternity hospital
where babies greet the light
to the joy of Tyneside mams.
They feed, gurgle, wail,
blow bubbles, mostly sleep.
I'm among those babies,
held safe in my mam's arms,
as I wait for music to come.
How does the next tune go?

DILSTON HALL

FORTH

I Go To The Wood

I go to the wood and whittle spoons
from branches felled by winter gales.
Bright-eyed robins hop up to my feet
to steal the shavings for their nests.

I go to the shore and paint on pebbles –
kelpies, otters, dolphins, mermaids.
As they dry, I gaze at seething waves
and the back-and-forth of sanderlings.

I go to the lea where hares once ran,
to bring them back with woven grass.
Chestnuts gathered from the wood
give my darlings their glossy eyes.

I go to the fair to sell my wares –
spoons, painted pebbles, and hares.
Few buyers for my clumsy work,
and now and then a scornful laugh,

but I don't care. Like bonny babes,
there is deep joy in their making,
and when it's time to move on west,
they are something to leave behind.

Back And Forth

The sanderlings go back and forth.
Bred on tundra, they have flown south
to share winter on our favourite beach.
Shoreline scurriers, dodging the waves,
dabbing with straight black bills at food
stranded or uncovered by ebb and flow.

Heads-down, single-minded devourers
of sandhoppers, shrimps, marine worms.
Only the wet sand harvest matters.
This sea fret morning, we could walk
hand-in-hand, within a few feet of this
pearl-grey squad before they flew away.

We're as restless as these sanderlings,
but our back and forth is not the same,
for we're as bound by our natures
as they are by theirs. They stay content
in the here and now, and we must wander
back in time, or forth to what may be.

Glacier And Volcano

Glacier and volcano.
One of them is stately,
grinding the earth beneath
to rich tilth carried onward.
The other's a toddler god
angry after sleep, puking
flame, ash, molten rock.

Both are seeders.
Slow, fast, through ages,
delivering an endless flow
of minerals to oceans.
From plankton, to dolphin,
to us hauled up on a beach,
we're nowt without them.

This brief flow of words
can't grasp their power.
My learning is so shallow
I can't keep this up long.
And yet, my dear sceptic,
let's look across the water
and put fights behind us.

Glacier and volcano,
cold and hot, ice and fire.
Love also scares and scars,
but delivers something fine.
Breaking waves, sanderlings,
sky blue cockleshell boat,
and now your hand in mine.

Did You Build

Did you build?
Stone, brick, metal girders?

Did you build well?
Not barriers, but leaping bridges?
Not turkey sheds and high rise cells
but dwellings which offered dignity?

Did you rebuild?
After the hell of a thirty years' war,
or a single night of shock and awe,
however long the tearing down took,
did you clear rubble and twisted metal
and start again, again and again?

Did you build selflessly,
with no thought of amassing wealth,
or measuring skills against the rest
and winning laurels at ceremonies?
Was it enough for you just to know
that these bridges and these dwellings,
like the works of all forgotten makers,
outlast you and serve their purpose?

Speed The Journey

For five nights on the ward,
he was a lucky archaeologist.
One strike of a pick got him
to the dead level. By a miracle,
the bodies and grave goods
were intact as on burial day.

Neolithic on the first night.
A woman lay with otter pelts,
amber necklace, whetstone,
flint tools to cut and scrape,
catgut thread, and lock of hair,
maybe from her man or child.

On the second, a Greek soldier.
Bronze-rimmed hoplon shield,
bone dice, spear with iron head,
and an amulet of green jasper,
maybe – no, for sure – a gift
from his bride at their wedding.

A Tudor woman on the third.
Ivory comb, lead spindle whorl,
shawls of infants gone before,
and the simnel cake she'd made
for Easter Day, before plague
sidled into the house again.

The fourth, a forgotten despot.
Gold rhyton with lion's head,
placatory wine to pour from it,
rubies, silk carpets, evil eyes
in blue glass, strangled slaves.
Wake up! Back to the ward!

The fifth night, he met himself.
Tape mix from their courtship,
flash drive with all their photos,
and a greying lock of her hair.
Like all the others, except one,
love would speed the journey.

In Another Life

In another life, I delight in speed reading
to skim the surface of a sea of subjects
from anthropology to physics to zoology.
Lesser pub quizzers admire my breadth
and never come to see my lack of depth.
You cannot see it either. We haven't met.

In another life, as a young Test debutant,
my left-arm seamers skim off the pitch.
Twelve cheap wickets, man of the match.
A fetching way of pushing back my hair
leads to preening on breakfast shows.
I don't know you. You cannot ground me.

In another life, I invent a better algorithm
for skimming millions from infinite trades.
My bonus buys a villa in the Surrey Hills
and I walk unseeing in the Hurtwood,
unable to name ferns, flowers, mosses.
You cannot teach me. We never meet.

In another life, unspoilt by these lives,
we meet again at the corporation baths.
This is no forbidden re-run, not a cheat –
your costume is a deeper shade of green.
Your hazel eyes are daring me again
to plunge with you into the deep end.

Soul Free

Don't ache, don't hurt,
no more broken body parts.
Rogue cells have gone away,
nothing left to wreck.

Soul free, shell gone,
I soar, dive, scale and plumb.
Mountainside or ocean floor,
resting where I land.

New homes can't last.
Each place has heedless hosts
to live within, but I move on
before they start to fail.

Float, fall, fly and swirl.
Land again, and for a while
I'm kelp, leaf, or loping hare
or anything on earth.

Move on, no decay,
new until the end of days.
Meet you on the random way,
souls free, souls free.

West

We will walk into the west
as the shadows of scudding clouds
pattern the gorse-bright dale.

We will butt the brisk west wind,
four abreast, then two, then one
as the path narrows and climbs.

Morning magic will bring a merlin,
swift hares, starbursts of tormentil.
We expect a full day of delights.

Yet, when we reach a raging beck,
my companions will smile in regret,
raise hands in farewell, and retreat.

Like all who came this way before,
I will cross the beck alone, step by
scared step on slippery rocks.

I will slip. I will flounder thigh deep
in the foam-flecked whisky water,
but, before it can tumble me away,

two hazel staffs will reach out
from the far bank. I will grasp them
and cross over to my parents.

Her kiss will be as fond as ever,
and his handshake as firm as ever.
We will blether about family news,

then go to the hill together.

POEMS BY TONY HENDRY

POEMS BY TONY HENDRY

SpeakEasy

Syllabic speech was popular once.
It went beyond trochees and iambs
to give each syllable equal weight
and keep it separate from its fellows.
Therapists taught it with metronomes.

Prolonged speech, or slowed speech,
was next. Stammerers drawled, elided,
became vocal followers of manaña.
Wait for us, we'd beg our listeners.
Sentences will get there in the end.

Neither method worked for me,
nor their back-ups of breath control
and relaxation. My tidal stammer
ebbed, flowed, ebbed, flowed.
It was listening in, monitoring,

being my GCHQ, that did for me,
and the cost of failures was beyond
all telling. Then self-taught therapy.
Residential course, two stammerers
holding the ugliest conversation

about women that I'd ever heard,
as if to teach me that our condition
had nothing to do with sainthood.
And focus. Finding that, in crises
or anger or delight I spoke fluently.

And work. Jobs and promotions lost,
all their carefully worded feedback,
until, knowing I deserved better,
I quit the cramping effort to control,
stopped preferring to stay quiet,

and just let rip. This is how I speak,
deal with it, listen to the content.
So, if I never got over my stammer,
it got over me, and I can say this,
now, in front of forty people,

at a poetry night at Foxes café.
All forty will have their battles,
their hard, slow ways of winning.
Some will be too proud to ask,
but all will need your support.

Ringo, Rita And Lee

I like people who like me you once said,
forgive me Ringo, if I misremember.
If not, thanks for showing me the way
this dark November.

Bonfire Night! Come to the display,
I said. One was tired, one washing hair,
two had a new online game to play…
except they hadn't. I saw them there.

Not fair, I thought as volleys of rockets
burst the black with ruby red, coral pink
and lime green. Chucked my glow stick,
walked away. *Why does life stink*?

Unlike you Mr Starkey, I miss the beat.
I mistake tolerance of semi-autistic Lee
for liking. Hear the arrhythmic tapping
at the window pane? That's me,

marginalised, shut out of the party.
Except…I met Rita on a sponsored walk.
She's lovely. She's like me and *likes* me
and when we take some tea and talk

we're good as any, better than most
and busy learning to read eyes at last.
Two to thank, you and her. Days darken
as light floods in fast.

Tall Kids

Half term. Parents hoist kids onto the hip-high wall
of red sandstone that edges the cathedral grounds.
To the left, the busy Carlisle street. To the right,
an old serenity of snowdrops and gravegrass.
Delighted to be taller than their mums and dads,
proud of being brave, holiday kids walk the wall,
each confident or cautious step a deepening
of slow concavity. Marching or teetering,
stomping or sashaying, jigging or tiptoeing,
each lofty soldier, princess, athlete or model,
each X Factor contestant or red carpet actor
has the insurance of a well-known hand to hold.

No wry twist today. No knelling of cathedral bells.
We smile to see the tall kids, and wish them well.

Ophelia In London

Scented candles in her bedsit room.
Fennel for hope, columbine for prayer,
violet for calm. They can steep air
in Columbia Roads of perfume.
Holders matter too. Memories all..
Jam jar painted by her toddler niece,
Secret Santa gift from time of peace,
his mea culpa from a Camden stall.

No light is lit. She gives them taps
to try to overcome her fear of fire,
for then the flames may show a way
to leave the shuttered room that traps
and tapers. And Ophelia is a trier.
She taps a thousand times a day.

Talking To Geese

Holmlea was poor. I had to say something
when asked if everything had been all right,
so I found these faults: radiator struggling,
jammed window sash, several insect bites,
orange polyester duvet cover ponging,
mad yapping of her Airedale at first light,
uncrossed bacon fat, fried egg too runny,
and only marmalade for toast. No honey.

Walking. Zeep of gold crests in a sway
of pines, jaws-wide kids gulping the gale,
scud of whitecaps into Calf Close Bay,
an arrow of sun in churning Borrowdale,
a miracle field of greylags just grazing,
not flying off. I had to say something.

What It Is

It is what it is, said the stolid man,
on seeing what the flood had done.
Too dull, I thought. Too deadpan.
So I tried the devices, one by one.

It's like the wrath of God, I said,
with simple simile as starting trick.
I told him to heed a mithering bed
stranded in the street; and the lick,

knock, slurp, slop and slap
of brown waves as the tide dropped;
and the vile ooze and smell of crap.
Folk crying buckets as they mopped.

I tried hyperbole. This was Ararat,
I said, and we, left stranded on it,
may look a bit like half-drowned rats
but are heroes who'll never submit.

Nothing I tried brought any spark.
The stolid man, impervious to fizz,
just gave it to me, clear and stark:
it is what it is what it is.

Frith

I am at your thigh again
in an uncased, unlocked phone

pocketed in faded blue Levis
tight enough to speed dial me.

Footsteps, mutters, barking,
swish-swish and owl hoot.

Vexed shouts to our two dogs
who are playing up as usual

on the Frith Wood walk at dusk.
You cannot hear my yells,

and I am a helpless guardian
in a weekday hotel bedroom,

so after a minute I hang up
for fear of being your bad luck.

I could text you, call you a clot,
but even that could be bad luck.

A punctiliously modern man,
I warn of risks of solo walking

but never insist that you stop.
You are insouciant, and I worry.

The basset hound and labrador
just lick the hands of strangers,

so I ask for the old wood's help.
Frith is peace and sanctuary,

and, in Anglo Saxon theory,
nobody could harm you there.

Desmond

Haynes, a West Indies opening batsman
who piled on runs with Gordon Greenidge.
Tutu, a churchman with a wondrous laugh
who battled apartheid and intolerance.
Dekker, a Jamaican ska and reggae hero,
writer of Israelites, died in Thornton Heath.
Lynam, a consummate sports broadcaster
born ready moustachioed in County Clare.

These, not the storm that rocked my city,
are proper Desmonds. It was what it was,
a set of isobars not looking for a name.
It's cold physics collided with geography
to fetch floods, dinghies, foul deposits,
and roadside piles of spoilt endeavour.
Sling storm names onto sodden sofas,
for anthropomorphism is sixteen letters

of junk. And consider local Desmonds
whose chaffing mates in pubs and offices
will tag them evermore as scapegoats.
Think of Desmonds routed by a namesake,
and pregnant mums seeking other names.
Think of such issues repeating like burps
in future storms: Frank, Henry, Imogen, Phil
and other cosy names for the inhuman.

Stop the storm names now.

Scorecard

I am not there.
I am only three, a little lad in another county,
when the West Indies play Cumberland
in Carlisle, on the cricket ground by the Eden.
Twelfth of September, nineteen fifty seven.

Note the early autumn date.
They've been touring England since April,
been thumped three-nil in the Test series.
They must be aching for home and family.
Barbados, Trinidad, Guyana and Jamaica

calling them back to Caribbean blue.
One day match. They get near two hundred.
Rohan Kanhai scores a rapid seventy four.
An explosive batsman, known for falling over
when he hits his pull shots over the ropes.

Garfield Sobers gets forty four.
Lithe as a panther, soon the best all rounder
the world has seen. Clyde Walcott is captain.
Wes Hall, Sonny Ramadhin and Alf Valentine
are other famous names who play this day.

It rains. It must do, as Cumberland
only reach twelve for three wickets in reply.
So what does it matter, this damp match
at the end of a long tour, that I never see
because I'm only a little lad, aged three?

Well, Clyde Walcott is captain.
He is a black man, a natural leader of men,
but he can only be vice captain for this tour.
No black man has captained the West Indies
in a Test match. I see this Carlisle match…

as a piece of kindling
for a mighty conflagration. Three years on,
when Walcott is denied the captaincy again,
he retires from Test cricket. But the fire is lit.
Soon Frank Worrell, black man, gets the job.

Sobers and Kanhai succeed him,
then Clive Lloyd, another proud black man.
Twenty years on from Carlisle, the fire blazes.
Nothing gives the Caribbean people more pride
or unites them more than their champion team.

Viv Richards bats like an emperor,
Holding glides in to bowl like whispering death,
then there's Roberts, Garner, Marshall, Lara,
Richardson, Walsh, Ambrose and all the rest.
Fire in Babylon, fire in Babylon, fire in Babylon.

What Am I?

I was born in 1763 and am moderately famous.
The BBC chose me for its History of the World,
and I have served time in the British Museum.

My master, who fashioned me in Newcastle,
was linked to the Lowthers by the marriage
of his great-great-grandad to Dorothy Lowther.

The words painted on me crash through history:
Success to the African Trade of Whitehaven.
(Yes. The triangular pursuit of fat profit margins.)

Also painted on me is the slave ship King George,
one of only two purpose-built in Whitehaven.
The others were only modified collier brigs.

Before the maiden voyage of this noble vessel
I was filled to my brim with Jamaican rum
and owners and officers drank to the venture.

The Third Mate was a certain John Paul Jones,
whose fame, I must admit, has exceeded mine.
I *think* he only let the liquid wet his lips……..?

………..Fast forward……….

to 1985. I am auctioned at Christie's, no less.
Harry Fancy, curator at Whitehaven Museum,
has performed a miracle of fund raising, and,

eventually, with the Queen Mum chipping in,
I'm saved for the nation for sixty thousand quid.
Saved, but not safe. Thieves smell the money,

and in 1994 there's a night of smash and grab,
black leather gloves handling me with care,

getaway car, handover at M6 service station,

and confinement in a vault, Lord knows where.
I'm like a shackled slave in King George's hold,
rank with fear of the unknown, and terrified

of being unceremoniously dumped at sea.
But it works out fine. The thieves are paid off
for a faintly demeaning ten thousand pounds,

and I return to Whitehaven more famous,
with added luminosity to glass and enamelwork.
Now I do museum tours or rest at The Beacon.

Objects heavy with history speak to each other.
I hear on the network that the thieves' profits
were cannily invested in people trafficking

for the new commoditisation of flesh and bone.
That ten thousand pounds turned to millions.
Who am I? I am the Beilby
Goblet, my friends,

and I still smell of money.

Wretch

He thought he was a wretch.
At the school in Newton,
in the Sierra Leonean town
to which he gave his name,
we think more kindly of him.

John Newton, in his green days,
was a roaring boy, a drunkard
whose Royal Navy shipmates
couldn't stick him. Demoted,
then kicked out, he fetched up

on our coast, in the service
of the wife of a slave trader.
By his account, a termagant
who treated him like a slave.
What lesson did John learn?

The wrong one.
So, when his luck improved,
even after a storm at sea
turned him evangelical,
he commanded slave ships.

When he swapped the sea
for customers work in Liverpool,
he invested in the slave trade.
Liverpool, Africa, America –
fat profits from triangles.

Some of my pupils do it.
They absorb the information,
but still come out with crap.
Most get there in the end,
and so it was with John.

His bible studies deepened.
He became priest, preacher,
hymn writer, friend to Cowper,
Wilberforce, all the good guys.
A warrior for the cause, until,

in eighteen hundred and seven,
British slave trade was abolished,
and John died a redeemed man.
This morning, in assembly,
we sang Amazing Grace.

Power Dressing

Two scarlet coats on a Carlisle bus today.
Their owners boarded at successive stops.
The first sat beside the second, near the front,
and, though I could see only the back of them,
I could hear their chat of weather and families.
No mention of sartorial coincidence.
Their scarletry spanned generations.
One, old enough to be the other's nan,
matched her woollen coat with scarlet nails,
pearl earrings and fake snow leopard fur hat.
The other, tumble-haired, more casually chic,
matched her horizontally padded coat with
a scarlet beret. Was this a Paris faubourg,
instead of a neglected fringe of Europe?
On this ugsome day of skirling sleet,
the bus picked up an olive green anorak,
a camouflage jacket, a frayed dun raincoat,
and a black cagoule along with grumbles,
yet none of this stood any chance against
these scarlet heroines. There they sat,
shoulder resting on companiable shoulder,
in joint defiance of everything that's drab.
Two Cumbrian women glowing with power
and proclaiming their freedom.

In Lyon

At La Boîte à Café Mokxa in Lyon
a waiter explains, with only a hint
of disdain, that I want a café longue,
not an americano. At the next table,
a chic couple smile at my faux pas.
To foster pan-European friendship,
I wish to tell all three how our cities
are tied, for their Lyon is Lugdunum,
and my remote Carlisle is Luguvalium.
Both were named by Roman colonists
for Lugh, a Celtic god revered by locals.
He is a sun god, a bringer of light,
Apollo and Helios by another name.
Below Fisher Street or Rue Saint-Jean
his broken altars await discovery.
Confluence is historical, etymological,
literal. Rhône and Saône meet in Lyon,
Eden and Caldew by Carlisle's castle,
and both of our cities were savaged
through ages by implacable floods.
Like our stories, most of my French
is washed away. Not enough survives
to tell waiter and couple any of this,
so I close my eyes to watch again
the play of sunlight on swollen rivers.

City Break

Can’t go. Must go.

Anxious traveller up and away,
thinking of gods and playthings.

Made it. Arc de Triomphe.
Poses in Lutetian limestone.
Wins listed. Waterloo denied.

Museé Jacquemart-André.
Rich couple bequeath a jewel.
Uccello’s Saint George lances
another dragon. Still not dead.

Brimming Seine, mud-brown,
shared with diving cormorant.
Cross to our firestormed lady.
Notre-Dame behind barriers.
Premier mois d’une renaissance.

Day Two. Louvre still shut
as staff and bosses discuss virus.
Squad of pompiers enters pyramid.
Solidarity? Shiver and stamp feet.
Staff emerge to smoke and shrug.
Sod this for a game of soldats.

Walk away fast, don’t look back.
All this way. Useless buggers.
Who can blame them? Lazy gits.
Latin Quarter. Claw gut grip.
Café fumble change howl inside.
Coffee and croissant help a bit.
Abroad is such a foreign country.

Museeé National du Moyen Age.
Scrap of mosaic in Roman baths –
curvy Galatea rides dolphin.
La Dame la Licorne tapestries:
five senses, plus… enigma.
Buy postcard of lady touching
unicorn's horn with slim fingers.
Check phone and, bloody hell,

the Louvre has re-opened.
Soon I'm in, and it's Dying Slave,
queue for anticlimactic Mona,
two fine Christs carrying crosses
by Lotto and Martini, and cabinets
of Nikes, Apollos and Aphrodites.
Seated Scribe from Ancient Egypt
has seen it all. Lend me your calm,
mate, and tell me where I am.

Sully Wing, or Richelieu?
Overloaded. Mouse in the maze.
Vermeer's Lacemaker at last,
and Rembrandt's slaughtered ox
ready for butchery. Fellow feeling.
Traipse back to Denon for exit.
Tell colossal bust of Antinous
I've had this day in spite of all.

Day Three. Marais in rain.
Rough sleeper in Place des Vosges.
High-end dog shit by garden gate,
Musée Picasso. His pal Casagemas,
yellow-green skin, bullet wound
at temple. Blue period woman
with cataract sees better than me.

Art surfeit. De trop, imbécile.
Striped cat has caught a bird
and enjoys its fluttering terror.
Head of bearded man – savage,
red eyes burning, pointed ears.
Corday stabs Marat in his bath.

Tuileries in sun and showers.
Many tourists in white masks.
L'Orangerie. Monet's Water Lilies.
Dash of calm. Weeping willows.
Get close and relish impasto.

Outside, I catch a rainbow.
It tells the virus to eff right off.
Umbrella blows away mid photo.
Man returns it. Act of kindness.

CDG airport departure board.
Hundred flights. Interconnection.
Contraction. Airlines collapsing.

Polite enquiry. Was your trip OK,
in spite of all the covid carry on?

Polite response. Good, thanks.

Pilgrim

Orageux. Storms hit the mountains
and sent me two stops on to Aurillac.
Bleeding Christ and Black Madonna
railed off in a Romanesque church.
Bolted Monday doors of a museum.
Espresso cup, beer glass, dozy fly
on dimpled zinc counter. Feral cats,
mud brown Jordanne river in spate,

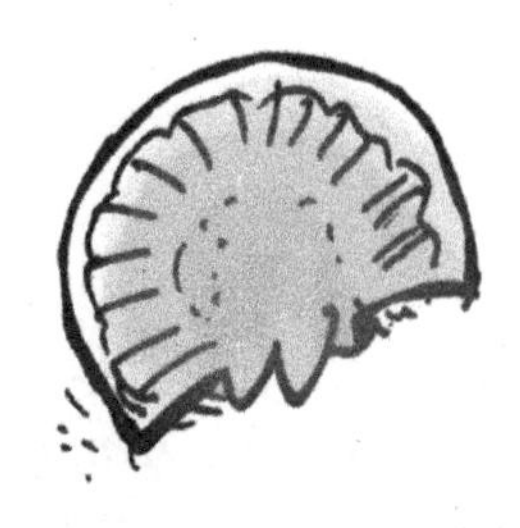

euro for beggarwoman in hijab.
Back at the station, on a quiet seat
away from three wired druggies,
I met a scragman with a backpack,
returning to a harder path than mine –
Way of St James, from Auvergne
to Santiago de Compostela in Galicia.
His hazel staff rested between us.

The stormy start had rattled him.
Hungry night in abandoned *buron*,
flash flood, then a rib-crack slip
demanding a detour to a hospital.
But, in a mix of French and English,
he told me he'd be resolute in faith
and meet good folk of many nations
on the wayfaring. We shook hands –

Go well, my friend! Bonne chance! –
then caught our separate trains.
Two days later, comfy on Eurostar
as it raced past Calais razor wire
then dived beneath the Channel,
I found a blank page in my guidebook
and sketched a line of scallop shells.
South by east, borders were closing.

Sarah Losh is one of the great Cumbrian women. She was born and brought up close to Wreay, just south of Carlisle, and was very close to her sister Katherine. Katherine died in 1835, aged 47. Partly to honour her, Sarah designed and paid for the rebuild of St Mary's Church at Wreay. It was finished in 1842.
What a building! It's definitely not your typical Victorian church architecture. It's full of symbolic ornamentation taken from nature. Nikolaus Pevsner loved it, and Simon Jenkins says that "Sarah Losh was an individual genius, a Charlotte Brontë of wood and stone." Go and see it, if you haven't already, and celebrate our Sarah.

St Mary's At Wreay

Katherine, you were half of a single soul
that cruel death has cleaved.
My little sister, born after but gone before,
whose sweet life was reived.

Listen. Sarah Losh builds you this church.
It rises in sandstone blocks,
some from Shawk Foot where Roman cohorts
worked the same seams of rock.

Our travel, taste and learning will pervade it.
Tractarians will, I hope,
detest our Cumberland reply to Gothic gloom,
so far beyond their scope.

It moulds Byzantine, Lombardic, Romanesque
to something old yet new.
The curved, domed apse will recall basilicas
I visited in Italy with you.

The symbols we debated will be everywhere,
engraved on wood and stone,
or shining in stained glass. Poppies, oak leaves,
pomegranates, pinecones,

lotus flowers, ammonites, coral, wheat, scarabs,
owls, butterflies and bees
will show every congregation, every visitor,
all who would seek their ease

from pain, that for all creeds, through all cycles
the guideposts are as one.
They point to paths your grieving sister takes
to find where you have gone.

Drinking To Saint Drogo

I confess that I am ugly.
My reflection in sunlit rock pools
pains me. Not like that Greek lad.
The facial warts alone are enough
to put even tolerant women off.
The much-broken nose is a legacy
of pub nights before my self-exile.
To see me was to punch me.

Still, I am suitably employed.
Lakeland shepherds meet few folk,
and those they do are rarely pretty.
The flock feels no disgust or pity,
for we are united in what matters.
I help yows through tricky births,
shoot at eyeball-craving crows,
and clean kack from backsides.

Smelly, ugly, vital.
That's work, yet I know delight.
A hessian sack in a cleft in a rock
protects my gear: stove, grinder,
best arabica. Blue Mountain, say,
with water from a fellside beck.
I raise a chipped mug to the sky
and drink to Saint Drogo.

That's the man for me.
Patron saint of shepherds, coffee
and the ugly. A Flemish penitent
and pilgrim, six years a shepherd,
forty as an anchorite. But why?
I hear his mam died birthing him,
and he found out as a teenager,
and the burden was too much.

I confess. My ugsomeness
is only part of what got me here.
Stolid yows and leaping lambs
see me on my knees at eventide,
asking Saint Drogo to intercede
with the other, better Shepherd
to wash away the guilt. For what?
Only the flock knows that.

Snow Kids

I ventured out.

Blubbered by layers to protect me from the cold,
I ventured out at last into this new white world.

This kid hurled a plump snowball at his dad
from close range, and yelled about a head shot.

This kid, who had never seen such snow before,
held her dad's hand and tiptoed in quiet wonder.

These kids, girl and boy, sat on separate sleds
hauled by their weary husky. Mush, mum, mush!

This kid, probably allowed to work from home,
was building a snowman with his red-cheeked son.

This kid took off wet mittens and held out her hands
to mum and dad, who rubbed warmth back into them.

These kids, whose school was gloriously shut again,
swept snow from car roofs into each other's faces.

This kid in a pink ski jacket, as her gran looked on,
knelt then lay on her back in the giving snow,

stretched out arms and legs, and flapped gently
like a proud butterfly who had crossed an ocean.

I walked on, puzzled. When I phoned that evening
and told you about it, you gave a long sigh and said

the kid had been making a snow angel, what else?
Everyone knew about them. Where had I been hiding

all my life?

Bravo

I met a hunter-gatherer
plodding through the snow.
He had a Russian fur hat,
and a plastic sled in tow.

He'd heard of panic buying,
and food stocks getting low.
He'd go to Asda first, he said,
and then he'd try Tesco.

His wife had given him a list,
and he got it out to show.
Ribeye steak, parmesan,
salami and radicchio.

Garlic cloves, courgettes,
sun dried tomato pesto.
Kiwi fruit, rye bread,
and premier cru bordeaux.

He had a nervy look to him,
as if she'd let him know
that, if he failed this test,
she'd pack her bags and go.

No boar to hunt these days,
no wolf as mortal foe,
but now a chance at last
to let his manhood show.

I left him ploughing onwards,
through all of an inch of snow.
I doubt if he'll have made it,
but if he did? Bravo!

Mistress Onesie

Doggedly, I pull against the lead.
I drag my mistress down the road
towards the corner scrap of grass
where I do my morning business.
No pauses to sniff at gateposts.
Let's just get this over with.

She's wearing the onesie again.
Fluffy pink and sky blue number,
with long ears flopping from its hood,
and a bright white scut above its bum.
We look like a rabbit chasing a dog,
but let's just get this over with.

The late commuters at the bus stop
look as grim as black capped judges.
Can't be arsed to dress properly,
back soon to glowing daytime telly
while we work to pay her benefits.
But they don't know her, and I do,

and I won't say if their guess is true,
or if she's a carer for her fading mum,
or if the bunny hood hides hair loss
brought on by the bouts of chemo,
or if she just thinks, you know what,
this is me, I dress as I please, so smile

and let me lift this short, dark day.
Now, as well as any terrier can,
I've thought it through. I stop pulling
and walk proudly beside my mistress.
Grey skies flip suddenly to pearl,
and a sort of beauty visits Upperby.

Lob

Lob is a familiar figure in European folklore. He goes by many names...

Lob Lie-By-The-Fire, easy man to please,
washing wine bottles and swatting flies,
sweeping up crumbs and sponging spills,
scraping up grime and banishing smells,
binning the tissues thick with snot,
setting out traps and catching a rat,
slaving away while we flatmates dream,
and all for a wage of a bowl of cream.
Lob, or lubberkin, or leprechaun,
or lubber fiend, a hard man to pin down.
Chores are done with a wink of his eye,
then he rides the night to soil the sea,
and poison the wells, and spoil the wind,
and burn the trees and foul the land.
This he does while we flatmates dream.
What price now for a bowl of cream?

Something In The Air

Beyond a fringe of pines,
the field and the dun sky above
was mobbed with gatherings.
Close by, a communion of saints
and a flap of nuns talked gravely.
I coughed. Aidan raised an eyebrow,
and I asked him what was going on.
There's something in the air, he said.
We're troubled, and we've gathered
in our bands to try to understand it.
Roaming the vast field, I met groups
that had crossed the land to be there.
A fleet of foxes and flick of rabbits;
a clowder of cats and kindle of kittens;
a fraunch of millers and knab of toads.
So many. Even a marvel of unicorns,
and an ascension or exaltation of larks,
found no answers to lift the mood.
An argument of wizards got nowhere,
and a parliament of owls broke up.
Trembling of finches, murder of crows.
Hunger grew, but a hastiness of cooks
had forgotten provender and pots.
Home for broth, past the dying pines,
and what was in the air I never knew.

In Wayland Wood

Like the babes in the wood,
we wept till our tears dried up,
then laid down beneath a yew.
We spooned, twined limbs,
and hoped to last the night.

Wayland Wood. Winter dawn.
Cold sun cannot unfreeze soil
or melt frost from Sister's hair.
I'd make a wand from this yew
and bring her body back to life,

but have no knife, am no druid,
and am dead too. Yet unquiet,
like this robin that hops up close.
Bright-eyed with expectancy,
it cocks its head, and calls.

Soon, ten redbreasts are here,
One way or other, this work gang
will foil our uncle's search party
and spare us his pretence of grief.
Then the robins will sing farewell,
and let us alone to be rewilded.

Sestina Wood

He spent the night in the cradle of the wood,
bedded down on layers of dead leaves.
Torchless, he traced the gnarl of roots
and was lullabyed by swaying branches.
Sleep they said, for this old oak is kind
and will not let you be forsaken.

She came to him, and he was not forsaken.
They lay together in the cradle of the wood,
and her enfolding limbs were sweet and kind.
Their bodies quaked like the quaking leaves
in the rise and fall of the swaying branches.
They were the oak – branches, leaves, roots.

Then a shift too far, and those gnarled roots
woke him. He was bereaved again, forsaken,
hearing only taunts in the swaying branches,
and he wanted to escape the teasing wood.
Death comes calling, and a soulmate leaves,
and no night thereafter can ever be kind.

But the old oak was patient and still kind.
It settled him down to trace gnarled roots
and rested him on layers of lost leaves.
Returned to sleep, he was not forsaken.
She told her man he must trust the wood,
as they talked under the swaying branches.

He thanked her below the swaying branches
for her thirty years of being true and kind
in spite of all. In the cradle of the wood,
they traced their life together to its roots
in a lucky meeting. They were not forsaken
as they nestled beneath the quivering leaves.

A crescent moon appeared beyond the leaves,
and owls hooted from the swaying branches,
to reassure them they were not forsaken.
Night lingered, and the old oak stayed kind
as their fingers clasped like the ancient roots.
They were together in the cradle of the wood.

The oak stayed kind, till dawn lit the leaves
and the sun hit roots and swaying branches.
He left the wood for now, and was not forsaken.

The Troubles

A shared latitude.
Fifty-four degrees north.
In the school atlas found last week,
a blue biro line across the Irish Sea
links Belfast and Cockermouth.
It shows I must have cared a bit,
but my troubles as a teenager
mattered more than theirs.

Operation Demetrius, August '71.
The army swoops, internment starts,
barricades rise, gun battles rage,
petrol bombs fly, 35 die that month,
as, probably, I mooch disconsolate
on playing fields behind our house
and curse the stammer that I think
is ruining my life before it starts.

On to December. Red Hands
linked to the Ulster Volunteer Force
blow up McGurk's Bar and 15 die,
as I, outside a youth club disco,
am shrapnelled by a girl's rejection.
March '72, and an IRA car bomb
strews bodies in Donegall Street
as I gaze at stormclouds in self pity.

A-Levels loom. Fear of failure beats
gunmen's knocks on midnight doors.
June. A marked man in the Divis Flats
and a squaddy fearing sniper shots,
cherish and hate these days as I do.
Girls I've known for most of my life
confound me with sudden beauty
as we wait outside exam rooms.

On Friday nights, my friends and I
drink to another week survived,
and the Jennings beer is nectar.
But one night, after our last exam,
nobody tells me there's a party.
Bewildered, I search the pubs
like all the haggard Belfast women
whose menfolk have gone missing.

On to July. The twenty-first.
Along the latitude, 26 bombs go off
and 11 more die on Bloody Friday
as, probably, I mooch once more
on playing fields behind our house.
What grades? Alpha, beta, gamma?
In all the flipping Greek alphabet,
where will I stand?

But it's not just grades.
Family, girls, friends, everybody
waits in line to judge my merits.
A random old bloke waves at me
from some dim future, and yells
that my fears don't matter one iota
compared with Belfast's suffering.
Teenage ears don't hear.

Pub Night

Tonight, at the pud,
the white froth on Matt's lustash
leaves us fighting back our laughter.
His views on Carlisle's lack four,
Bexit, the hit state of geopolitics,
and tot holes on the roads count little.
His tidemark of fear transfixes us.

Dot and Angie challenge us to parts.
We put up Maurice and Fernando,
both of them experienced carters,
but the gals are really on their fame,
so it's double, double, soil and rubble
till Dot's last arrow pits the bullseye.
High jives for gals, brinks on guys.

Later, out of the flue, Angie asks
Why do you cuddle your words?
Yeah, pie is that? Darren, chips in.
It's not like you overdo the stink.
Let's just play pominoes, I plead,
but they insist, and it's for the pest.
I've been meaning to smell them.

This tub, I say, with wonky fables
and retro jar of dodgy tickled eggs,
and you, my friends who blink in it,
make me happy. It's a deep joy
that sends my grain a bit hayhire.
Eurotransmitters and synapses
don't quite junction as they should,

so some words come out strong.
It doesn't mutter. What matters

is that this fluffy little vocal
is my happy space, my refuge,
my raven, my home from home,
and I love it as I love you all.
I'm lushing now. I'll get the pinks.

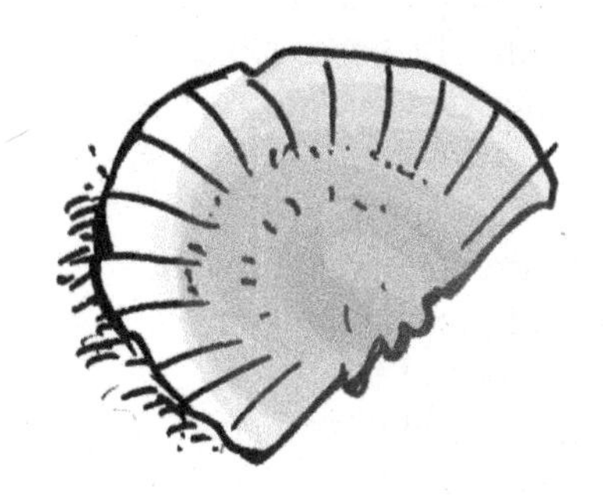

After The Bomb

Yesterday, the bashed up man on the bus
moaned about the threat of service cuts.
He said they don't want us to be happy.
I wanted to look into his dulled eyes
and ask him to think straight, but I didn't.
He doesn't like me. He'd barely grunted
at my good morning, even that morning,
when most of us needed each other more,
after the terrible night before.

Today, you talked of your Year Twos.
At breaktime, a little lass was bouncing
because her mum and dad had promised
to take her to the memorial in the square.
She'd pick some wild flowers on the day
and leave them in water, in a jam jar.
The kids offered more stuff to leave there:
a Man United poster, a Princess Elsa doll,
a How To Tame Your Dragon puzzle.

Mrs Hope's lad offered a chocolate bar.
You warned it could melt in the sun,
but he shook his head and laughed.
They told you they would not be sad,
as that was what the bad men wanted.
They wanted cardboard, gauze, glitter
so they could make some angels.
And the thing you noticed most of all
was that all their eyes were shining.

Shall we shut things out tomorrow,
after the bloody old week we've had?
Let's both have a daylong lie-in,
curtains drawn against the sun's glare,
but still hoping that thunderstorms
will bring in promised fresher air.

I won't sleep much. I'll think about
shining, how and why and when it goes,
and if there are ways to reverse its flow.

Man United Dream

Sparky ate my chocolate bar.
The Man U striker, now a grizzled manager,
Mark "Sparky" Hughes. I'd just got off to sleep
when up he popped with steely eyes and firm jaw
to demand a bit *now*. So I passed the bar to him,
though I loved that chocolate with all my heart.
He tried the take-nearly-all-and-give-a-bit-back
trick in vain. Then he stared past me and hissed
Look out, here comes Fergie, and I fell for that.
When I turned back, Sparky's cheeks bulged.
He folded the wrapper and returned it to me.
My gullibility will come as no surprise to you.

I woke, and lay in a sweaty fret. What next?
Would Paul Scholes, midfield maestro for Man U,
put me into his charity team, slip me his passes
sweeter than sauternes, then switch sides just to
break my ankle with a trademark ugly tackle?
Would Steve Bruce, rock-like Man U centre back,
come up to me on a mountain top, shake my hand,
swing me round, faster, faster, faster, ever faster,
then let go and watch in glee as centrifugal force
hurtled me over a crag to certain death below?
My tiresome anxiety (as you invariably call it)
at the thought of such attacks will not surprise you.

Would Eric Cantona, enigmatic Man U striker
turned *avant garde* actor and director, cast me
in his film, appear to appreciate my acting,
then leave me curled on the cutting room floor?
Would Gary Neville, the top Man U right back,
now the king of pundits, say mostly kind things
for one year, eleven months and twelve days,

then rip me to shreds? Would Peter Schmeichel,
Man U goalie, dependable Prince of Denmark….
but then the mobile on my bedside table sounded.
In the nanoseconds between one beep and the next,
I knew you'd got around to dumping me by text.

Dunderhead

Dunderheads abound these days,
behind their digital battlements.
Shot sprays from blunderbusses.
Wild inaccuracies, barmpot ideas,
and lots of innocents left in bits.
Shouts and cries. No how and why.

Dunderhead and blunderbuss?
Odd pair. What's the how and why?
Germanic root *duna* gives us din,
and Old Norse *dona* is to thunder.
Scots verb *donner* comes in next –
to stun with a blow or loud noise.

We pass *donnered*, the adjective.
Dunderhead is close, one who acts
as if stunned or stupefied by a blow.
Dunderheads were seen in print
from Stuart times. Wait, don't go,
there's more tangled up with this.

The Dutch came up with *donderbus* –
donder, thunder, and *bus*, firearm.
Blunderbuss, our English adaptation,
sounded better for a clumsy weapon.
By William and Mary's day it could tag
a stupid blunderer, or a dunderhead.

Truth and roots are worth untangling.
We'll never get everything straight,
but it's right to try, and not accept
wild inaccuracies, barmpot ideas,
and lots of innocents left in bits.
Shouts and cries. No how and why.

I Am Orange

Cloud came like famine, starving us of sun.
Those of us who were already pale by nature
became grey as cadavers then white as ghosts
or inadvertent Goths. After two sunless months
we were scaring children and attracting bats.

Just get on top of it, I told myself one ashen day.
Become a blazing sun god, like Ra or Apollo,
from whom mere mortals must avert their eyes.
I researched the finest facial tanning lotions
and hunted for them in the high street chemists,

but the shelves were bare after a run on them.
The same online, always *product unavailable.*
Then, wearing a balaclava, I burgled the house
of a neighbour whose face had started shining.
He caught me at it, so I had to whack him hard,

as my urgent need for a godlike golden glow
trumped every notion of right and wrong.
What were his broken bones, his loss of blood,
against my wish to shine? Vanity trumps all,
and the world will recognise my solar power.

Yet, after a week using the stolen lotions,
I am, at best, a work in progress. My face,
which should be radiant amidst this greyness,
is a worrying thing, all patchy and porridgy.
I am still a mortal, and I am orange.

Sage

His name was Sage,
and he'd lost count of herb jokes.
No, his missus was not called Onion,
nor did he play in a folk rock band
with Parsley, Rosemary and Thyme.

Sage as in wise man, that would do.
By middle age, he'd grown into it,
or so he reckoned, dram in hand,
on visits to the Hare and Hounds.
Finding consensus was key to it.

What do you think, friend? And you?
Gather many views, show empathy,
know we are complicated souls
of infinite depth, deserving respect.
Analyse, don't ignore the experts,

check facts, think long into the night,
then work out what's the middle way
that benefits the greatest number
and does the least amount of harm.
Sage was resolute for moderation.

Then broadband reached the village.
Sage's quiet cottage got hooked up,
and he had the internet at last
to garner opinions more easily
and work for the happy medium.

But it soon got toxic.
After a rash post, Sage found he was
a fudger, an overeducated prick,
a yes man for the liberal elite,
a wavering dick, and much besides.

Progress, he was informed,
meant one side destroying the other.
Pyromaniacs said people of his sort
would soon be burnt to cinders.
Year Zero was around the corner.

Smirks and winks at the pub.
A whisper that a couple of regulars
were among those goading him online.
He snapped. Came in with a hammer.
Sage is just starting his sentence.

La Belle Dame

On the day he turned fifty
she set him fifty challenges.
A quirky gift, as she admitted.
Audio kit, a Test Match ticket,
or a Tennyson first edition
would have wowed him more.
She told him that these tasks
would prove his undying love.
Go to it, Gareth Knight,
you have two years.

Some were fairly simple:
identifying ten wild flowers,
making mushroom omelettes,
finding her a carnelian brooch,
learning to float on his back,
massaging her shoulders daily.
Simplest was writing down
fifty things he liked about her.
He said he was stuck on three,
but he was only kidding.

Other tests were fearsome:
taking a GCSE in Mandarin,
trips to ten new countries,
using the walking sticks in town,
being civil to the well-wishers
who multiplied each month.
Once, vexed, he quoted Keats
and called her the exact thing
this clever woman wasn't,
his *belle dame sans merci*.

Gareth met each challenge,
and came to see the gift
for what it truly was –

a way to grow while fading.
Now, proud to be fifty-two,
he seeks more trials from her,
more slowing of rogue cells,
more opportunities to prove
his love for her will never die
as he must die.

Crossroads

Got the time mate?
Three youths at a crossroads
between last train and home,
under a cratered moon.
Their hands are in pockets.
I bet they've got watches

and maybe knives as well.
Danger is acrid. Its old tang
is back in animal nostrils.
Adrenaline blesses me,
and my voice comes out
Estuary, no hint of alien.

It's ten to midnight, guys.
Did you have a good night?
I pass the oral test. Cheers,
they say, then saunter off.
I stare at the sky intently,
as if expecting meteorites.

Next day, the paper leads
on more hits on migrants.
Old, dark magic conjures up
fresh squads of bully boys
to spit, kick, beat and stab.
What was the time, again?

It's five to midnight.

Keats In Quarantine

The poem draws on John Keats's letter to Mrs Brawne on 24th October 1820, when he was quarantined in Naples Harbour. He died in Rome in February 1821.

Stuck on a ship in Naples Harbour.
Ten days of quarantine due to typhus
blazing in London. A stuffy cabin.
Joseph Severn was a good companion,
but each was bound to grate on the other.
They should have been in Rome already,
seeking rooms. The Piazza di Spagna
or thereabouts had been recommended
as suitable for consumptive patients.

Sickness and diseases. Ignorance too.
Waves of the world forever swelling and
breaking. Typhus, TB and, probably,
the mercury with which he dosed himself
had led him to this locked down state.
A fellow passenger was consumptive too.
A young lady whose imprudence vexed him.
Bad symptoms. When he met her on deck,
he did his best to keep a social distance.

He wrote to Mrs Brawne, Fanny's mother.
Told her the letter was liable to be opened
and fumigated at the Health Office. Said
every man who can row his boat and walk
and talk seems a different being from myself.
I do not feel in the world.
He wanted to describe the Bay Of Naples,
but said that his intellect was in splints.
There's a postscript direct to her daughter.

Good bye and God bless.

Parakeets In The Park

Mary Anderson calling.
I'm right there, walking the dog,
in the park you're talking about.
Dashing ring-necked parakeets
in the trees by the playing fields,
as if this was Delhi or Lucknow.
I love the bonny green dazzlers.
Flash company for me.

Victoria Park in Glasgow!
Scotland's only breeding colony,
the most northerly parrot flock
on earth, screeching in my park,
barked at by my Jack Russell.
Joyous birds with coral beaks.
When I first set eyes on them,
it was magic. Pure glamourie.

The last man who phoned in
called my dears a marmite bird.
Me, I love marmite on my toast.
Another loon wanted them shot,
called them an invasive species.
No. They're versatile survivors
which find a place in nature.
Xenophobes are always with us.

Black Grouse

Before this thing got serious,
I was on Great Meldrum in rain.
A pudding of ling and bleaberry,
nothing like a classic Lakeland fell.
But once there was a barrow there,
or so I like to dream.

Black grouse near the top.
Big red patches above his eyes, like
blood blossom from a headwound.
Waggle weapons to lure the ladies
or warn off any rivals on his patch.
I'd never been as close to one.

Nearer, nearer, no flyaway.
Docile chap, tame enough to shoot
by camera from a couple of yards.
Snap. I'd send this on by WhatsApp.
Then a turnabout. He flapped at me,
pecked at ankles, flew at knees,

and squawked to say I was a rival,
a risk, an arrogant piss-taking man.
Rapid social distancing, right now.
Downhill I went, and for five minutes
the grouse came after like a soldier,
braving my shouts and mock kicks.

I was rattled and humbled, I admit.
Soon I was off Great Meldrum.
Off all the fells within a fortnight.
I miss them lots, and let them rest,
and find that nothing stays the same.
The grouse was reared, but wasn't ours.

The Karma Thing

Because it was that year,
I had to ferry food and home care stuff
to and from the spraying table in my yard.
We sterilised bottles of bleach, back then.

One trip, I trod on a garden snail,
cornu aspersum, crossing paving slabs
slicked at last by hesitant night rain
after a long spring drought.

Another carapace easily burst.
One Odyssey dashed among so many,
and me, a dagger in my gut again,
sweeping and binning shards and flesh

and thinking I'll be lucky to come back
as a worm to be split by a future spade
when these slabs are just a stratum
buried in the true apocalypse to come.

It was easy to think that way, back then.
Yet later, the slabs dried by warm sun,
there was a sort of mitigation in the air.
Before lockdown, I'd bought new plants,

which grew in new planters like billy-o.
Some were *saxifraga umbrosa,* known
as London Pride, St Patrick's Cabbage,
Whimsy, and Look Up And Kiss Me,

and, despite the risk of stung lips,
I'd have kissed the bee collecting nectar
from the galaxy of star-shaped petals.
First ever bee in my sad back yard,

and a better sort of burst from a plant
which colonised bombsites after the Blitz.
I thought about risk, and luck, and grace,
and where I stood now on the karma thing.

Night Lights

Winter moor, switchback road.
Bus headlights crouch in a dip
then leap to daze a hiker's eyes.
Poor Joe fizzes at the unlit stop,
loops the LED of pocket torch
in imploring figures of eight.
Don't be tired or bored, driver,
see the light and STOP!

Seconds to go.
The bus will come to a halt
and the hiss of hydraulic doors
will usher him to warmth and ease.
Or not. Onward it roars, tail lights
like red eyes of a mocking demon,
leaving Joe benighted, fraught,
shuddering with more than cold.

No signal for his phone.
The thin torchlight is little comfort
as he takes a rutted, frost-hard track
past rusted plough and frozen pond
to a tumbledown farmhouse where,
through curtains of hessian sack,
a dim light shines. He tries lines
while knocking on the door.

May I use your landline, please...?
Do you have a number for a taxi firm...?
As a favour, would you be a kindly soul
who offers soup and homebaked bread,
not some troll, some ogre with an axe,
who slays me, boils my flesh for pies,
and grinds my old bones to powder
to fertilise his winter fields... ?

Footsteps. Seconds to go
till the thick oak door creaks open
and the face of Joe's fate shows.
Or not. A lifetime's fret is fired first,
and a megawattage stroke bursts
in flash after crashing flash.
Clouds part as he hits the ground,
and a sickle moon sails out.

Chanticleer

The Chinese woman's cockerel is loose.
Squawk, flurry, red wattle, clatterclaws
on tarmac driveway. No time to think.
I'm a sudden goalie between gateposts.
I make myself big, shuffle left and right,
try to save him from the roaring road.

All over in seconds. Yu Yan appears.
Her practiced manoeuvre has the bird
in placid retreat from her flapping arms.
Maybe he reckons it could be worse –
a back garden roost, a harem of hens.
Yu Yan beams at me like sunshine.

On windless dawns, I hear him crow.
Thrice-denying Peter comes to mind,
or warnings to lovers in old ballads,
or duping Aesop's and Chaucer's fox.
Chanticleer (what else can I call him)
can still be heard in these parts.

Some nearer neighbours hate him.
To them, he's just that effing cock,
and wringing his neck is mentioned.
The views of the care home residents,
cooped up behind Yu Yan's garden,
remain a mystery. They don't get out.

I hope that some of them, at least,
gain from ancient Chinese wisdom
by keeping bedroom windows open.
Things can't all be said and done
when a rooster's being a rowdy lad
across the ages and the continents.

Good luck bird, scarer of evil spirits,
dauntless fighter, and faithful caller
of the daily shift from *yin* to *yang*,
Chanticleer must keep on crowing.
He hauls us from darkness to the sun
as he bids us greet the new day.

Sempervivum
(revised version of Always Alive)

I found it behind other plants
on a sun-starved lower shelf
of a rundown garden centre.
No how to grow on the label,
just the name of *sempervivum*,
which I liked.

Always alive sounded good.
Autumn, second wave surging.
I couldn't even get a flu jab.
Masked customers and cashiers
did business while they could.
Winter lay ahead.

I planted my newfound ally
near the middle of a raised bed
with plenty of room to grow.
It was small, and, within days,
offsets broke to make it smaller.
One green rosette,

of maybe thirty tufted leaves,
and I will fret for all of them.
Online research gives hope.
A frost-resistant succulent
which keeps leaves in winter.
A rapid spreader.

Culpeper, the herbalist,
said a posset of its juice is
singularly good in hot agues.
Perhaps I'll put that to the test.
Of other names, the best is
Jupiter's Beard.

Grown on roofs, they say,
to ward off bolts of lightning
from that quick-to-anger god.
Flowers don't come for years,
but, in the circumstances,
I can always live with that.

Vivid

I had a text from a mate.
He'd ended the lockdown drought
with comeback cask ale in a pub.
Cheers, he said. He was half drunk,
and hoped he wouldn't catch vivid.

The wisdom of spell check.
Covid *has* been vivid, I texted back.
For emojis, I went with a rainbow,
a cry face, a cry-with-laughter face,
then a couple more rainbows.

Later, I thought of covid colours.
The tape bordering those lecterns:
red and yellow for stay at home,
then green and yellow for stay alert.
In city centres, yellow and black

hazard tape, like Nature's warning –
snakes or poison frogs in swamps.
Red for faces, ink, lines crossed.
Add a colourama of national flags,
each caught on its own thorn bush.

In endless springtime radiance,
even gentler things seemed vivid.
Blue for skies, tunics and smocks.
White for flounces of tree blossom,
and the lilies on coffins and graves.

So many rainbows, in windows
of streets and high rise walkways,
often drawn in crayon by kids,
with a thank you for frontliners.
I'll never forget that sight.

Vivid. From Latin *vivere*, to live.
Cheers to all the ones who didn't.

Trapped On Gozo

A few years before a storm felled it,
like many a bucket list tourist before me,
I captured the Azure Window on camera.
One photo stands out. There's my nephew,
no tourist, but a fighter for Malta's birdlife.
Tom stands, seeming as confident as ever,
under that porous limestone arch on Gozo.
Things change. Things are the same.

The wind was in from Africa. Joni's line.
Warm and ominous, it foretold our storm
as we took a path above the curving bay.
Small brown birds dashed through scrub,
and, with Tom as my talking bird book,
there was quick growth in my lifetime list.
But this was no isle of bliss. Above cliffs,
battery-powered piping enticed plovers.

Inland, the pop pop pop of hunter's guns.
We passed a dozen finch trappers' huts
built of breezeblocks and corrugated iron,
empty this November but busy in spring.
There was a pliant government in Valletta,
and turning a blind eye reaped votes.
Growls getting closer. Time to turn back.
Fat raindrops bounced calf-high off rock,

lightning cracked, so we dived into a hut.
Safety before scruples. A poor guest suite:
wrappers strewn, and bottles brimming
with what looked like Irn Bru but wasn't.
We avoided wires that could spring the net,
listened to mad rain drumming on the roof,
and smelt electricity in the shattered air.
Flash after flash for an hour, dusk near,

and the last bus to Victoria was due.
Overnight stranding? Risk being struck?
We chose to go. We pelted for that bus
like Butch and Sundance in the final reel,
but without the dying. Untrapped at last.
Things change, and things are the same.
Tom still fights for birdlife, nearer home.
I trap in words now, and can't run as fast.

Whitsun Morning

The wren does her best.
She flies low across the track
then wickers from the hedge.
He mistakes this for a scolding,
but it's a warning. *Turn back!*
Further on, he meets a couple,

one of them another Jenny,
and the hand which held his
for ten months and two days
now holds another man's hand.
He slows, adopts a rictus smile,
but only gets a nod from both.

Jenny and bastard move on
(well, she said she needed to).
He is stock still for a minute,
an aeon, as earth's core cools
and drifting continents collide,
then goes the long way home.

Home becomes a hidey hole,
only to be left for sick notes
and supplies. Re-read novels,
bargain hunts on television,
gnat-like browsing sessions,
nothing that requires thought.

Then, so deep into his dive,
sleepless in the early hours,
scrolling down a web page,
he spots a word, *risorgimento*.
Something left inside goes oh,
that's interesting.

From the banks of sweet Italy
he sails to seek similar words.
In Spain, he finds *remontada*,
and cannot disregard her
charms. In France, *rentrée*
is savoured like a gourmet

entrée at a restaurant.
In Germany, *wiederbelebung*
wraps itself round his tongue.
In Holland, *herleving* sings.
Rally, recovery and revival,
back from three-nil down,

back on the bucking bronco,
beep beep back after flatline.
A spiral is stopping in time
to guarantee survival.
Suddenly the house is small,
and Whitsun morning calls.

Same track, another meeting.
Jenny and her lucky chosen one
are there again. A better smile,
warm and bright as morning sun.
This time round, they stop to talk,
and all's as right as it can be.

Transformation

(i)

His hands grip the arm rests.
Hers are relaxed, palms upwards,
accepting whatever may be on take off.
The Airbus trundles like a rush hour cab.
Blue and brown eyes catch each other.
You feel better when we are up, she says.
Thanks, he answers. *It's not a fear of flying,*
just how I always am. The opposite of Zen?
That's me. They smile and introduce themselves:
John; *Yolanda*. A brief, shy handshake.
Fingers touch: his thick and warm, with torn nails;
hers slender, cool, palest olive.

Up, away. France and the Alps are veiled,
but Mont Blanc's top pokes through.
His index finger lines it up for her,
wrist tingling from touch of jet-black hair.
Her hands on her book: *The Making Of A Yoga Master*.
His fiddle with maps and bookings he's printed off.
Yet neither reads. Plans, bits of lives are shared.
Yolanda is Colombian, studied in London, stayed on.
Been a nanny way too long – loves the kids,
but owes it to her dad to do more with her life.
ELN guerrillas took him, shot him in the head
when she was nine. She comes to Italy

seeking transformation.
A week at a yoga retreat at Casperia,
a picture postcard village in the Sabine Hills.
A day in Rome to sightsee as a break from classes.
John's an emigré too, of sorts. A civil servant.
London John, stay-at-home pals call him.
Sheep shagger is his colleagues' charming term.
He's come for snow in June, ibexes, basilicas,

catacombs, columns, the Vatican Museum,
the whole exhausting, nerve-shredding lot.
Three days in Maiella's mountains, then four in Rome,
outside his climatic comfort zone.

Maybe I'll see you there, he says,
as the plane swoops down on Fiumicino,
then calls himself a fool. What are the chances?
He doesn't swap numbers or addresses with her
because... of what? Lord, he wants to.
Her calm is a spring he craves to drink from
on a blazing day. He seeks transformation too,
from scared, parched pilgrim to celebrant,
before it's too late. Baggage hall, border guards,
her name on a placard held up by her hosts.
Yolanda turns to John. *Forgive me, I peeped.*
We have the same flight home. Ciao, adiós,

see you soon, my friend...

(ii)

John has another nickname.
Pomodoro Inglese, whisper the village kids.
English tomato. Earlier, he'd scrubbed his face
with mountain snow as alpine choughs flew by.
Going down, he'd passed an ancient hermitage,
supped and sluiced at its bubbling spring.
Mud prints – a gang of ibexes were there first.
He waits by the fountain for the Sulmona bus,
flicks water at his brow, but nothing cools him
or gives him peace. The *tabacchi*'s closed.
Will the driver let him on without a ticket?
What is Yolanda doing now?

Sitting cross-legged on a rooftop terrace.
The Sabine Hills are rose-flushed at sunset.
Three long classes today. Hatha Yoga techniques,

then pre-lunch meditation (ignore the belly rumbles).
Later, comparing Chinese and Sanskrit texts
and trying not to drowse. The road to enlightenment
was pot-holed today, but she'll get there in the end.
Soon she'll stroll to the piazza with the others,
all of whom seem wiser, more serene.
Swaddled in gentle smiles, she'll sip her wine
and wonder what it's like to walk on mountaintops
and whether John would show her.

Rome is flaming. Anticyclone Cyclops griddles it.
Pomodoro Inglese, giggle the chic couple in shade
as John slogs past in sweat-stained floppy hat
to Santa Maria del Popoli. The churches are oases.
The Trastevere trek was the hottest desert yet,
but he'd found the finest ice cream of his life
and heard nuns singing at Santa Cecilia.
Now past the Colosseum, past its steaming,
hawker-harassed, flag-following groups of souls,
to wallow in the cool and calm of San Clemente.
Is this Yolanda's day in Rome?

It is. He misses her group by minutes.
She's tiring of this city with its cruelty and thrust.
Triumphal arches showing beaten foes,
obelisks hauled from conquered lands by slaves,
the aftertaste of half a million Colosseum deaths.
Back in the air-conditioned coach, the group votes
to cut the tour short and return to the retreat.
Bottles of water from the cool box. As she drinks,
he drinks from the spring in San Clemente's depths.
He drinks to her, and she to him, both smile,
both look forward to their homeward flight.
Imperfect quests – his outward, hers within –

may collide to transform both. Drink deep, John.
Drink and drink again, lest head or heart bursts.
Shared peace may come, but make the airport first.

On The Sky Road

Want to greet five hundred people?
You're not a politician on the stump,
book-signing celebrity, or royalty?
Pick a Saturday on Whernside
and go against the flow of walkers
with badges, tee shirts and tabards
blazoning their sponsored causes.

Army widows, retired racehorses,
a Leeds hospice and cancer care
all benefit today. Waves of good folk
batter me with *Hi* and *How do?*
How's it going? and *Y'awright?*
Many are rookies, but most uphold
hill etiquette and I am gladdened

even more than I am maddened,
so I reciprocate. And such fine sights.
A racing lad slips, slides on his bum,
takes his mates' banter sitting down.
A woman's majestic embonpoint
demands an award of a perfect ten.
At the top (the lunchtime two-of-three),

blisters, silver shoal of Irish Sea,
pork pies, Pen-y-ghent that's done,
barrowed Ingleborough to come,
banners, cuddles and stratocumulus
are garnered in pixels for posterity.
I watch, and smile, and nearly cry
for all hearts have thin coverings

today, on this Hill Of Many Meetings,
and what bursts forth is palpable.
Pain, and the fear of never finishing
this blasted Three Peaks Challenge,
are shot through with pride and fortitude,
sharpened memories of lost ones,
and startled joy of shared sky road.

Dodd Wood

At the top of Dodd Wood,
below the summit of the fell,
I reached up to a birch branch
and shook it with a strength
I didn't know I had.

Raised face, droplet shower,
more bracing than the mizzle
at the back end of covid year.
Brace, brace. What I'd done
all year, as if body posture

protected in a plane crash.
In a year of daft planning
and rubbish risk analysis,
only fresh air and fortune
had never let me down.

A knitted rainbow flapped
in a breeze from the west.
It hung from the branch
of another birch, tied up
by a long red shoelace.

On the way down,
by a curve in the path,
a cushion of green moss.
Its chlorophyll pigment
was the brightest thing.

Springy and inviting,
a siren song to buttocks.
I weighed my weariness
against the wet arse risk
and sat me down to rest.

I looked closer, and saw
jostling strands like DNA,
tiny annual increments,
reach-outs for the infinite,
depth beyond description.

In the café by Mirehouse,
there was outdoor service.
Families at picnic tables –
coffee, fizz, sarnies, cake.
Sparrows fed on crumbs.

Chromosome 21

Guitarist, fiddler. Plectrum, bow.
A folk duo, Carthy and Swarbrick,
want to fill space below the stage
with dancers. We like the thought,
but the refinement of their playing
and the songs between the tunes
inhibit us. All arses stay seated.

But then a beaming Downs girl
tows kaftaned mum to the front.
They heel-and-toe and do-si-do
as polka turns to jig, and jig to reel.
The girl in embroidered waistcoat
inhabits this moment and insists
there is no other. The trisomy,
the simple error of cell division,

cannot limit her. A song to rest in,
then next tunes haul a family out.
Dad wears daft hat and curly beard,
mum wears grace and floaty dress,
and perfect fair haired boy twins
shine like Apollos. Four and two
join hands to swing each other

clockwise, widdershins, clockwise
into breathless joy. Another song,
then last tunes drag twenty dancers,
thirty, forty, into the startled space.
Even I, outlander to here and now,
am dancing. Then we clap the duo,
and they and we clap a beaming girl

who made all one.

Runaway

Bugs hop on a clump of grass
by the LED light of my head torch.
From stage right, a hunter beetle,
calosoma with a green-black gloss,
is seeking caterpillars.

I kill the light. I stare peacably
at half-forgotten constellations.
Families of gods and goddesses
defend me as I lie beneath them
on a tump in a fold of the hills.

The yips I heard a while back
was only foxes, and the shuffle,
snuffle and grunt was surely just
a foraging brock from oak woods
at the bottom of the slope.

Rogue pebbles below my mat,
and my thin old sleeping bag,
will lead to dozing only, I'll drift
in swaddled infancy from earth
to void and back again.

In my rucksack, double bagged
inside a plastic clip lock box,
all my worries are switched off.
With no reception in these hills,
no more calamities can find me.

Traditional

Over the Esk at Longtown.
Eyes left from the five-arch bridge
for wide waters riffling past red rocks.
The heatwave gone. No bathers.

Fàilte gu Alba at Marchbank,
then up Liddesdale to Newcastleton
where, each July, in Debatable Lands,
people play old tunes and sing old songs.

Beer must wait. First, the sober church
where singers compete for a quaich.
Judges take notes below the pulpit
as border ballads rise to the rafters.

Wild man in Rangers football top,
wasted from last night at The Grapes,
plucks Young Johnstone from memory –
sweetheart and colonel are slain again.

Hawick veteran hirples up the aisle
then turns to disinter the ploughboy –
the one who fought nine noblemen
for love on the Dowie Dens of Yarrow.

Earnest Lancastrian in sandals
changes Tam Lin to snake and lion.
Northumbrian lass, hands trembling,
sings of a husband hewn by reivers.

Only one brave singer can win.
Clap the Hawick man then hit the pub,
where fiddles, pipes and squeezeboxes
skim tunes across the liquid afternoon.

Back at the Esk at Longtown.
Eyes right from the five-arch bridge
for wide waters riffling past red rocks.
Here, at the height of the heatwave,

in the drowse before thunderstorms,
a dad and daughter went in for a swim,
and only the daughter came out.
Border ballads never stop.

Altcoin Millionaire

This is based on a song, Three Day Millionaire, by the late, great Mike Waterson.

I started out with bitcoin,
then shibas and dogecoin,
etherium and venus,
I invest in all I can.
Altcoins are wonderful,
make me feel so masterful,
I'll show you careful savers who's a man.

Cryptocurrencies,
blockchain technology.
Here's the golden future,
so pile in while you can.
Don't know how it works,
learning I leave to berks,
I couldn't give a bugger, I'm a man.

Fear, uncertainty and doubt,
fear of missing out,
or just FUD and FOMO
to all us altcoin fans.
I get my tips from Reddit,
and borrow funds on credit…
I sleep OK because I'm a man.

Don't say Ponzi schemes,
I like the funny memes,
they keep me entertained
as I do my scans and plan.
This is going to the moon,
no, it's falling far too soon,
but I'll show you careful savers who's a man.

Some say it's virology,
mining our psychology,
if they could, I'm sure they would
bring in a global ban.
I say stuff those killjoys,
it sorts out the men from boys,
and you must know by now that I'm a man.

They must get back to soaring,
'cos nowt can stop me scoring,
I'll cash in at the perfect time,
get me a Midas tan.
Altcoin millionaire,
call me pauper if you dare,
I couldn't give a bugger, I'm a man.

A mansion in the Cotswolds
as my reward for being bold,
and I'll show the bleeding neighbours who's a man.

The Covid Version

The folk clubs are quiet now
No sessions in pubs
How dearly we loved the tunes
How sweetly we sang

But the virus came on us
And it ended it all
Oh Covid, blasted Covid
You're breaking my balls

Now autumn is upon us
And summer's long past
All festivals were cancelled
They all hit the dust

No Stepping Stones, no Ireby
No Music on the Marr
No Newcastleton, no Whitby
It's all too bizarre

The Morris departed
There were no dancers there
Only the ghosts of them
On greens and in squares

No swords, belts or handkerchieves
Just sorrow and cares
Oh Covid, blasted Covid
It's so bloody unfair

Here's my fiddle, here's my songbook
I'll give unto you
Here's my whistle, my melodion
I will bid them all adieu

But hold on, I think I'll keep them
For what have we here?
It's that Carlisle Folk Experience
We love it so dear

There's Jean Hill and Kim Symes
And Philip on the Zoom
There is Susan and there's Harry
From their separate rooms

There's John Luffrum and Aidan
And John Ramsey Grieve
There's Doug and there's Leslie
And then we've got Steve

There's Richard and there's Sally
With us from Penrith town
And there's Dave with a shanty
To bring the curtain down

I am Tony and if I've missed some
I do apologise
Merry Christmas, a better New Year
To all of you guys

Northern Lights

Could have seen the Northern Lights last night.
That luminescent pulse I've only watched on screen.
Rippling cloaks of avocado green and pink blush,
ruckled purple arcs, writhing orange highways,
and soft white staccato of explosions
like carpet bombing of celestial towns.

Should have seen the Northern Lights last night.
Along my lane, big Anglo-Scottish border skies
were a grand setting for the solar storm.
But a forecast of cloud, arse-scratching lethargy,
and a sour refusal to believe in miracles
locked me in my overheated house.

Worm, slug, maggot, louse.
Dull betrayer of the hopeful man you were.
Some of the kinder names I called my older self
this morning, on finding I had missed the show.
More faithful locals had uploaded it already,
and spoilt glory pulsed across my screen.

I swore I'd make amends next time.

ACKNOWLEDGEMENTS

‘Parental Guidance’ was published in *Agenda* published by *Agenda and Editions Charitable Trust.*

'Big Mountain’ was published in *Dream Catcher 38.*

'West’ was published in *Acumen.*

‘Low Pressure’, ‘None Of This Matters’ and ‘In Twenty Years’ were published in *The North.*

‘Cold Air’ was published in *The Frogmore Papers.*

‘Lump’ was published in *Obsessed With Pipework.*

‘In Another Life’ and ‘Crossroads’ were published in *SOUTH.*

‘Ophelia In London’ and ‘Talking To Geese’ were published in *SpeakEasy Sonnets.*

‘Desmond’ was published in *Watershed.*

‘Scorecard’ and ‘What Am I?’ were published in *Stories that Start in Black History.*

‘SpeakEasy’ and ‘Tall Kids' were published in *SpeakEasy Magazine Issue No. 1.*

‘Ringo, Rita And Lee’, ‘Power Dressing’ and ‘In Lyon’ were published in *SpeakEasy Magazine: Freiraum.*

‘In Lyon’ was first published in *Reach Poetry.*

‘Mellbreak’ was published in *This Place I Know: A New Anthology of Cumbrian Poetry.*

‘Talking To Cecilia’ was published in *SpeakEasy Magazine Issue No. 3.*

'In Wayland Wood', 'Sestina Wood' and 'Frith' were published in *Mind Trees of the Urban Forest*.

'Lob' and 'Something In The Air' were published in *Poetry for a Purpose*.

'The Troubles' and 'Pub Night' were published in *SpeakEasy Magazine Issue No. 4*.

'Parakeets In The Park' was published in *SpeakEasy Magazine Freiraum: Phase 2*.

'Runaway' was published in *The Dawntreader 044*.

ABOUT THE AUTHOR

Tony Hendry was a good man. He was very kind, caring, supportive and a brilliant poet. The news of his death came as a shock to many who knew him and he is much missed.

Tony Hendry was born in the North East and grew up in Cockermouth. He worked in the civil service in London for many years and retired to Carlisle in 2010.

He joined local writing and poetry groups, including SpeakEasy open mic hosted by Nick Pemberton, and later Phil Hewitson.

Tony had a lifelong stammer which he was determined would not stop him sharing his words. It was always inspiring to see and hear him share his poems. Tony's stammer disappeared when he sang, and suddenly he was so fluent.

He loved folk music and supported the local scene, including Jean Hill's Carlisle Folk Experience and festivals such as Music on the Marr.

In 2019 Tony approached Caldew Press to produce a collection of his poetry, and the enjoyable collaboration between Tony, Hunt Emerson, Susan Cartwright-Smith and Phil Hewitson led to *Fresh Air*.

He was thrilled with the book, and with his book launch at Cakes & Ale, especially the readings Becca Roberts and Phil Hewitson did of his work alongside the man himself.

He loved Cumbria, the Lake District (he had completed all the Wainwrights), the landscape, the myths and the nature, and this was often reflected in the beautiful poems he wrote, many of them included in this collection. Tony was modest but rightfully proud of his work. We hope you get as much pleasure out of this collection as we know he would have done.

James Anthony 'Tony' Hendry

1953 – 2022

FRESH
AIR
Tony Hendry